Finding Your Fit & Building The Relationship: *Online Dating*

A Guide for Seeking Your Best Match and Developing a Healthy Long-Term Relationship

By MARCUS NOLON MIMS

ISBN: 978-0-578-59690-7

This book is dedicated to my son, Nolan N. Mims, parents, Hazel and William Mims, and all the other wonderful relatives in my life that were role models and examples of what loving relationships was all about.

Contents

Preface

In 1988, I became divorced. Free from the married life and back to the single life. Like many other newly divorced men around my age at the time, I returned to the dating scene attending house parties and other social events. Yes, I was back into the arena of being available.

While attending many of these social events which I met women of all shapes, sizes, professions, and characters; surprisingly I was not finding that special woman that I wanted to have a long-term relationship with and possibly marry. Despite my divorce, I enjoyed the marriage life. It was comforting being in a committed relationship and doing things together as a couple. When I divorced, I knew I would eventfully remarry, but I was not going to get into another relationship that would not be a good fit for me. Therefore, I needed other options for finding that elusive desirable woman, other than just attending dances, parties, and other social events.

During the late 1980s, there were no online dating services around or at least, none that I knew of and even if there had been, I probably would not have joined based on it being an unknown. However, I did at the suggestion of some friends join a video dating service named Great Expectations. Founded by Jeffrey Ullman in 1976, the local establishment I became familiar with in Chicago was located near the Northside of Chicago; it was set up like a video library. After joining the organization for an inexpensive fee, I had a video of myself made for showing to the opposite sex. In the video, I talked about myself and what I was looking for in a mate; same as one would do in today's online written profiles. Weekly, I visited the office to view video profiles of women that interested me and leaving a brief message to those women whose video profiles captured my attention. Great Expectations would send me a notification by mail on how to reach those women that responded favorably to my greeting after they reviewed my video profile-greeting.

There were a few other competing video dating sites around during this time such as Teledate and Introvision and possibly a few others that were smaller and obscure. But, at the time, this was innovative matchmaking before online dating site concept became popular approximately in the mid-1990s; during the same period of the Internet explosion.

Flashback to today, there were over 2,500 dating sites in the U.S. with more than 1,000 new ones popping up annually. Some of the new ones had a short life span due to the competition and failure to get a high volume of members. Some of the new ones that survived were bought out by the more established and successful online dating sites. However, even some of the established dating sites tend to get bought by other competing online dating services. For example, as of 2018, New York-based IAC owns Match Group Inc, which includes Match.com, OkCupid, Plenty of Fish (POF), Tinder, and several others. As a result, Match Group Inc. had 1.7 billion in revenue in 2018, according to Statista, a German online portal for statistics. With successful and profitable numbers like that, there is no surprise that Facebook in 2018 decided to get into the online dating business.

For some time now, Match.com has been the most successful of dating sites in the U.S., and as of this writing, it still is. They are not successful because they were the first online dating site in the U.S. created in 1995; they are successful because of the large size of their membership, their ability to attract new members, and most importantly maintain a database of compatible members that are pleased with the company services. Other dating sites are also successful at this, but Match.com is the leader and usually appears at the top of annual survey lists of pinnacle dating sites.

The largest free online dating site is Plenty of Fish followed by OkCupid at the time of this writing. The numbers of users are in the millions. It's those kinds of numbers that keep more users logging in to find the woman or man of their dreams. New users come and go daily, while others remain on the site for several years. I was once among those repeaters that remained on Plenty of Fish and Christian Mingle. I met some wonderful women and had some good times while on dates. Some of those relationships lasted for quite a while, but none were serious enough to lead to marriage.

Later, after becoming somewhat disenchanted by the lack of finding that special someone; I decided to develop a tool and strategy that would guarantee that I would eventually find the best match for me among the maze of women out there on dating sites.

The approach involves identifying one's values in terms of what they desire in a relationship and taking those factors and assigning numbers to them for calculating on an Excel Chart. I named it the Compatibility Point Factor Chart. The higher the rating, the greater the probability that a person will be a better match for you. I have used this chart as a key to determining what women I would consider approaching online. If they did not equate to a certain high number of points, then I would not even bother to contact them.

The Compatibility Point Factor Chart works because you are weighing your potential mate with values that are important to you. The more that person has similar characteristics that you have, the more both of you are potentially a better match.

Whether you use a paying or free online dating service, you want to make sure you are utilizing your money and time wisely and not just blindly going through several profiles not having a game plan or approach that assures you a high rate of success. The bottom line, the Compatibility Point Factor Chart helps you achieve success in finding your match.

There is so much more covered in this informative and helpful relationship book. For example, there is a chapter that helps singles post profiles that strategically assist them in attracting potential compatible partners. There is a chapter that summarizes some of the best dating sites for finding long-term relationships as well as a section on some reasonably new dating apps and websites. Readers will learn what factors to consider before going into a long-distance relationship. There is information on how to both build and retain a healthy relationship once you found that special someone, whether online or offline. There is also information and thoughts about both dating and marrying outside one's race; and a chapter that helps singles determine whether or not they are truly ready for marriage or remarriage. Also, if they are prepared for marriage, there are several suggestions on how to make their marriage successful.

Those that are serious about finding their soul mate online should consider many of these methods and ideas I present in this book. Also, once you identify your potential significant other; you should quickly take the relationship offline so you both can get to know each other away from the distractions of the online crowd.

Note that the primary focus of this book is for those using online dating to seek long-term heterosexual relationships, including those that may lead to a possible marriage. Also, if you are new to online dating, this book is a perfect resource for you. If you are using online dating for casual dating, friendships, or same-sex relationships, this book would not directly apply to you, although some of the concepts, ideas, and suggestions may still be useful to groups with such intentions.

Now we all know nothing in life is guaranteed other than death and taxes. What I can assure you is that the methods I share in this book, if used correctly and consistently, will help increase your chances in finding a compatible match. It will also present you with ideas and practices to help grow your relationships into something long-term and special. Afterward, the rest will be up to you!

Chapter 1

Six Factors that Identify Your Potential Match

Online dating sites can expand your dating and mating search opportunities. These websites can be especially helpful to people with limited chances of meeting others, such as working singles, busy single parents with limited free time, or those unable to find their match the old fashion way; at parties, bars, and other social events. One of online dating most significant advantage is that it allows you to meet others that you may not have met otherwise. Whether these people live near or far from you, Internet dating opens up vast prospects of potential matches for you.

However, to be successful in the online dating market, it's essential to first take inventory in what you are looking for in a partner. Not only will this better prepare you to write your online dating profile, but also help you to become more effective in selecting a match that meets your priorities and core values.

Although many significant factors can signal compatible relationship potential, the six key elements to look for are physical attraction, uncompromising needs, chemistry, values, friendship, and compatibility.

Physical Attraction

There are some exceptions, but for the majority of us, to connect with a potential mate, it is necessary for you to have some level of physical attraction toward them. Of course, mental attraction plays a role eventually, but we are referring to the initial stage of viewing a potential partner online. There physical presence is the first thing we see and is what initially captures our attention as we scan through their photos online. The mental and other forms of attraction may come later when we read their profile or actually communicate with them via written, phone, video-conference, or in-person conversation. Of course, the opposite could occur as well. For example, after reading through their profile and finding several factors we dislike about them, although the physical attraction may be still there, it's not at the high level it previously was before learning more about their character and other traits.

The point here is generally it is the physical attraction that first draws us to someone. Therefore, when we see someone online that looks appealing, many of us almost instinctively are attracted to that person's appearance regardless of whether or not they are a good match for us. It is the physical attraction that captures our attention and determines whether we want to identify that person as a potential match.

Also, what's physically attractive to one person may not necessarily be physically attracted to another person. That old saying "beauty is in the eyes of the beholder" is true.

Note that physical attraction is more than just being beautiful or handsome; it also involves proper grooming and hygiene. For example, a woman's natural physical beauty can be diminished or hidden if she has a bad case of facial acne. The same can be said for men.

It could be argued that men put more emphasis on physical attraction than women. To some extent, this is true. For example, many men do not take an interest in a woman's inner qualities alone. Generally, men need for physical attractiveness in a woman is a priority.

Women also require physical attraction in men but maybe not as intense as men. However, in the online dating world, the physical appeal is what both male and female generally turn to first in their search for a mate. It is for this reason; selecting photos for your online profile should be done carefully, especially the primary or principal photo on your profile page. This is the photo that will cause the viewer to stop and review your profile more thoroughly because of your attention-grabbing and attractive main photo.

Uncompromising Needs

After identifying someone that we are attracted to online, the next step we also naturally consider is whether or not that person meets those needs that are important to us. Or another way of looking at this factor is whether or not the person has elements that you won't compromise on. For example, you dislike smoking and therefore, refuse to date or get involved with a smoker. This automatically eliminates that particular person from being a potential match for you. Yes, you may still be physically attractive to the person's photo, but that physical attraction somehow lessens as a result of discovering that he or she is a smoker.

Therefore, our uncompromised needs can play a crucial factor in identifying our potential match. Other examples of uncompromising requirements we look for in a relationship include someone that is emotionally stable, mentally matured, dependable, responsible, and honest.

It is fair to say that without someone meeting our top needs, there is no possibility of that person being a potential match. Many of the desires that we hold dear are what make us who we are and is why we won't compromise on them. Therefore, acknowledge those needs that are vital to you and make sure at some point you determine if your potential match measures up to your uncompromising or most essential needs. But again, these are not just a wish list of requirements; these are must-have needs that you won't compromise on because they are important to you and are essential to your happiness and contentment in a relationship.

Can a potential mate learn over-time to meet your most essential needs? Why, of course! But during the dating or courtship period, don't expect that to happen anytime soon. Just as it takes time for a smoker to kick their smoking habit, it may take quite a bit of time for them to adapt to meet your must-have needs. And just like relationships, there are no guarantees that they will be able to meet your uncompromising needs. Therefore, sticking with those potential partners that already share your most critical needs is the preferred preference.

Chemistry

Like your uncompromised needs, chemistry cannot be overlooked when searching for your potential partner online. It is a reliable indicator of relationship success. It attracts people to each other, almost magic-like.

The better you understand how to notice and listen for chemistry in the dating process, the higher the success you will have in deciding if a person you find charming and desirable, is a match for you.

One of the critical steps in identifying chemistry during the dating process is to understand that your values create chemistry. Our values are our rules of conduct; they are the essential elements that inspire our actions. When we are connected to them, our efforts are natural and energized. And when we don't have chemistry with a date, interacting with them becomes somewhat more of a chore.

When it comes to chemistry in relationships or dating, relying on your gut feeling about someone is not enough.

Yes, your intuition or gut feeling is worth listening to and not to be totally ignored, but you need to have more direct contact and communication with that person for more reassurance and validation that real chemistry potential exists and that both of you may be a terrific match.

Different kinds of chemistry should not be overlooked. There is attraction chemistry, communication chemistry, comfort chemistry, sexual chemistry, much-in-common chemistry, and other forms of chemistry. It is fair to say that the more types of chemistry that you have with a partner, the stronger the relationship.

Although some forms of chemistry are not always immediate. Sometimes it can be developed over time during the dating process after couples have gotten to know each other better. For example, sexual chemistry between a man and woman initially may not be as exciting. But after the couple learns to react and respond to each other sexual desires better, the level of mind-blowing physical sexual chemistry increases.

Many online dating sites use written questions or tests to determine member's chemistry makeup. This is a reflection of how vital chemistry is a factor in helping to identify potential partners that are your best match.

Values

Another factor to look for in a partner during your online search is a potential mate that share similar values. Does that person share the same or similar values that you hold? Of course, depending on the comments they state in their written profile, not all the time, it will be obvious what values they have. This is why dating or meeting those you find as a potentially good match should be your goal when joining a dating site. Entering a dating site and not meeting potential compatible partners online makes the online dating experience less productive.

Avoid spending an extensive amount of time scouring profiles and only interacting with potential partners electronically. Schedule a date, or as some refer to as a meeting, with those that you connected well with online and have seemingly strong match potential. The dating or meeting process helps to not only assess whether you share similar values but also allows you to get to know each other better in other ways.

There are different kinds of values that we hold firmly. For example, many are passionate about their family, religious beliefs, and political values. Such needs would also fall in the category previously discussed concerning uncompromised needs. Those values that we hold dear are often challenging to compromise on. So, knowing what your potential partner values are can be critical in searching for a long-term relationship partner. The more aligned you are with your potential partner core values; the more likely you are bound to be successful in a long-term relationship with that person.

Friendship

At the core of any relationship should be a deep and strong friendship. What are common to many couples that have been together for a long time are strong friendships. They are best friends, and it is among the many qualities that keep them connected. Therefore, as you search online for your potential partner, ask yourself could that person you found interesting become your best friend and why. Initially, you will not know this, but after a few communications and productive dates, you should have some idea whether that person is "best friend" potential as well as a possible soul mate.

While our physical looks may change as time passes by, strong friendships among couples help to keep the relationship glued together. Besides, the love of your life should be your best friend. Ask many couples that have been married for an extended length of time, and they will often tell you that being best friends is one of the essential qualities that has kept their relationship strong. Therefore, ensure that those you date in your efforts to find your soul mate has the potential of being your best friend.

Compatibility

If we were to weigh all the above factors into one, it comes down to compatibility.

Strong compatibility among couples generates from having similarities in lifestyles, beliefs, and values. The more compatible you are with a potential partner; the more likely are your chances of being successful in a long-term relationship. Compatibility among couples tends to be what bonds them together. Without harmony, couples would be in constant conflict with each other and inevitably it can jeopardize the relationship.

Being compatible with someone will maintain a healthy relationship because you both are on the same wavelength. This will make for ease of making big and small decisions and not to mention a more successful relationship.

Compatible couples can't help from feeling a sense of unity. When you have couples that are physically attracted to each other, and they also share similar core values; they almost instinctively become interested in each other during the dating process.

How Chemistry Differs From Compatibility

It should be noted that compatibility and chemistry are not the same. Chemistry, as indicated early, is vital in a couple's relationship, but without having compatibility, it could jeopardize that relationship from being long-term.

Chemistry is composed of subtle conducts and temperaments that positively respond to the other partner. Couples that have chemistry tend to have a special connection when they are with each other. Such couples have emotional makeup that brings out feelings of warmth and excitement. However, chemistry, unlike compatibility, does not necessarily have the higher potential of a long-term relationship.

Chemistry is essential if romance is to occur, but eventually, the intensity will mellow down. This will cause the relationship to be re-evaluated and ultimately compatibility will be the determining factor of the relationship success.

For example, a woman who has high morals and lives a clean and healthy lifestyle may have great sexual chemistry with a drug dealer who also happens to be a drug addict. Eventually, the sexual chemistry will lessen as a result of the couple having different values that make them incompatible and ultimately ending their relationship.

What does this all means? Well, if you are looking for a long-term relationship that may also lead to marriage; give more weight to your potential partner compatibility with you than mere chemistry alone. Even if there is little chemistry but more compatibility between you and your prospective partner, the relationship still can survive. However, if there is low compatibility but more chemistry, the relationship is unlikely to survive long-term.

All of these factors will be very helpful in you identifying your best match during the dating process, whether it's online or offline. Some singles online profiles will actually give some indication that they may match you in certain areas. This could be reflected in their written profile or even a photo or two of some activity they are involved in, such as a photo of them playing tennis or riding a horse.

Know Who You Are and What You Want

If you are to use these factors effectively, it's essential that you know yourself and what it is that you want in a relationship before joining an online dating site where you will see a variety of different people with their own interests, values, and agendas. Going online to search for a potential partner without having an idea of what you are looking for in a mate, is like going on a strange road trip without a map or plan on how to get there.

Decipher what is really important to you so that you may align yourself with a person who truly complements you.

However, you may already know what you want in your search for a long-term relationship, but somehow putting it in writing tends to validate it or make it more real. So, the next step would be to come up with a written "wish list" of what you are looking for in a mate.

Key Points to Remember or Act Upon

- To be successful in the online dating market, it's essential to first take inventory in what you are looking for in a partner.
- The six key factors that signal relationship potential are physical attraction, uncompromising needs, chemistry, values, friendship, and compatibility.
- Avoid spending an extensive amount of time scouring online profiles and only electronically interacting with potential partners. At some point, schedule a date or meeting with those that seem to be a strong potential match for you.
- Acknowledge those needs that are vital to you and make sure you discover if your potential match measures up to your most essential needs.

Chapter 2

Knowing Your Non-Compromising Needs From Your Compromising Needs

Many singles searching for a mate already know what they are looking for in long-term relationships, but not many put those desires in writing. As referred to earlier, when you write them down, they seem to have more meaning and purpose. Therefore, list specifically what you want in a long-term relationship.

Uncompromising Needs

Starting with your most essential needs, you want a list that focuses on those needs that you must have in a relationship if there is going to be any possible consideration made to a potential partner of interest. These would be your deal-breakers. For example, if someone you are interested in on a dating site does not have your essential needs, the deal (potential relationship) is off. They are not considered a possible match. Here's an example of a list of uncompromising needs of a 50-year-old divorced white woman:

1. I need a man that seeks a serious relationship.
2. I need a man that's honest and has integrity.
3. I need a man that's a Christian.
4. I need a man that is single or legally separated.
5. I need a man between the ages of 45 to 55.

The above woman needs list can also be used in writing her online dating profile. Although not every item she lists may require inclusion in her profile, certain things such as looking for "a partner that's honest and has integrity," would be worth including, as among others listed items. Such a list of needs can surely make your written profile task much more manageable. But the primary purpose of a needs list is to identify what one seeks in a relationship. It keeps you targeted on such desires as you scan through online profiles searching for your compatible match.

Realize that some of the people you are attracted to online may not be able to measure up to all your essential needs. And even though such needs are considered uncompromising, you may want to rethink whether some of those critical needs can be moved to a more flexible compromising needs list. For example, maybe a person on a dating site meet most of your essential needs but happens to fall short on one of them. Still, however, you are attracted to that person and are willing to pursue them as a potential match. In such a situation, you need to reevaluate that particular uncompromising need that person did not measure up to because you are still willing to consider them as a prospective mate. You may want to remove that essential need from your list or move it to your compromising needs list. The logic is if you are willing to compromise on your uncompromising needs, then it may no longer be an unyielding need. It may no longer be a deal-breaker.

Therefore, limit your essential needs list only to those needs that are not to be compromised. If you find yourself compromising on anything on that list, you need to remove that particular factor from your essential needs list. But again, consider adding it to your more flexible compromising needs list.

Compromising Needs

Although your compromising needs will not be as valued as your uncompromising needs, they are still key factors to help you identify your potential partner. A list of this kind will also provide you with some options to determine whether someone you view on a dating site is a worthy prospect to communicate with and further your assessment of their compatibility to you.

Let's, for example, take a 35-year-old single black man seeking a mate on a dating site. His compromising needs list may look something like this:

1. I need a woman that cooks well.
2. I need a woman that enjoys sex.
3. I need a woman that likes to travel.
4. I need a woman between the ages of 25 to 37.
5. I need a woman that is either a Liberal or Democrat.

Again, compromising needs are flexible but still desirable. For this particular person, such requirements listed would not be deal-breakers. But they would if they were listed as uncompromising needs. So, it's essential to distinguish your compromising needs from your uncompromising needs accurately.

When you develop such lists, they help in identifying what we value most and what we are willing to show more flexibility. In the above example, the man sees a woman profile online that he is physically attracted to, but she lists in her profile that she's a terrible cook. Because the man is still willing to consider her as a potential partner is a good indicator that his need for a woman that can cook well, is not a deal-breaker or an uncompromising need.

As you develop an uncompromising and a compromising needs list, you are likely to find yourself making changes, and that's okay. The key is to be true to yourself by making sure each list accurately identify what values or needs that are most important to you and those that not as important.

Going on Dates to Get Answers to Your Needs

As many already know, dating is a two-way street, including online dating. Meaning, although you may show interest in someone on dating sites, they may not always share the same interest in you. So, when initiating contact with someone on a dating site, send either two or three messages at the most. If you failed to get a response from them, then move on. The person in their quiet way is signaling to you they are not interested. So, don't waste time on those that do not respond to you after two or three greetings or messages. You don't want to become annoying or harassing. Move on to someone that does respond.

Many of your needs will not always be identified in a potential partner profile. Often, both men and women online written profiles can be brief and include generic or "cookie-cutter" information such as short sentences regarding their interest in music, travel, recreation, etc. Although this type of information is worth knowing, it does not provide details on who they are and what level of compatibility they have with you, other than for example, similar taste in music and recreation activities.

It is when you start communicating directly with that person online that you begin to learn more about them. After a few written online introductory conversations, you will want to move the discussions offline via telephone or even consider having video conference calls to get better acquainted with them. If after a few phone or video conference calls you find that you have a connection or share at least a reasonable level of needs and interests, the next step is to schedule a date. A date or meeting will allow you to see each other in the flesh and have more direct and personal conversations that could either lead to future dates or interactions. It can also help determine for whatever reason you don't want to purse each other further. Or despite not having romantic interests in each other, you may still want to stay in touch as friends since you share similar interests in recreation activities such as tennis or chess.

Again, the dating process is for getting to know a potential partner. It is through these direct in-person interactions with your prospective partner that will allow you both to get to know each other. Therefore, make sure the date include some time for revealing conversation. For example, a date can be playing miniature golf or attending a movie; but make sure time is allotted to have some sit-down time, such as dinner or lunch for good conversations. Such opportunity allows you both to look at each other and read the other's reactions to your discussions.

Dates are not a time to be dishonest with each other. You want to show your true self. Putting up a false front that tries to make your date believe you are someone you are not is a waste of time. The more honest you are with each other, the better you both can determine if you are a potential match. You want to show each other your real personality and character so you can decide if you are a good fit. I believe, for example, if on your second date you have not yet determined what some of your date's political views are, don't be afraid to either directly or indirectly bring up politics; especially if a particular type of political affiliation is on your uncompromising list.

However, reframe from turning the date into an interrogation meeting. Be conversational in your discussion mixing fun, or playful questions with serious inquiries. Avoid having your date feel uncomfortable or annoyed by non-stop imposing personal questions.

Remember, the focus should be to enjoy each other's company while also learning more about one another to determine if you want to continue to pursue each other further. Also, the more dates you have, the more personal questions you may feel comfortable asking one another.

If after dating once or twice and you have determined that the person is not a good match for you, be polite and let them know that the connection is not there. However, wish them success in finding a more suitable match.

Online dating is somewhat like a numbers game, the more connections or dates you make, the better are your chances of eventually meeting your future soul mate.

In the next chapter, we will expand on the use of the needs list so that it is a functional tool for increasing your success rate in identifying a potential compatible partner for you on dating sites.

Key Points to Remember or Act Upon

- Realize that some of the people you are attracted to online may not be able to measure up to all your essential needs. You may want to rethink whether some of your uncompromising needs are actually your compromising needs.
- When initiating contact with someone on a dating site, send either two or three messages at the most. If you failed to get a response from them, then move on. The person in their quiet way is signaling to you they are not interested.
- Dates are not a time to be dishonest with each other. Show your true self. The more honest you are with each other, the better you both can determine if you are a strong potential match.
- If after dating once or twice and you have determined that the person is not a good match for you, be polite and let them know that the connection is not there. However, wish them success in finding a more suitable match.

Chapter 3

How to Develop and Use a Compatibility Chart to Evaluate Matches

Regardless of the type of dating site you join, you will find people on them with a variety of interests, personalities, ages, races, characters, shapes, sizes, quirks, and other unique characteristics and behaviors. Your objective and challenge as you search for a long-term relationship are to find a potential partner that's compatible with you.

Not only are you seeking someone that you are attracted to physically, mentally, and perhaps spiritually, but you also want to ensure that as you get to know that person better through conversation and time spent together that they meet many of your uncompromising and compromising needs. You also want to learn whether there are true friendship and chemistry potential between the two of you.

Many people on dating sites, especially the frustrating ones, will tell you it's not easy to find a compatibles mate online. However, that can be debatable. If online dating sites have a large enough number and variety of members and you search thorough enough, you are bound to find someone that's a potential fit for you. Dating sites members come and go. New members join almost daily, and many times, past online members return to explore or view the new crop of potential partners that are available online.

The key is to be patient and put in time and effort to search for those that meet your interest. Also, to increase your chances of meeting someone, consider joining more than one dating site simultaneously. This generally exposes you to more potential partners that capture your interest. You will sometimes see some of the same people on different online dating sites. Some single people put themselves on several dating sites to enhance their chances of finding Mr. or Ms. Right. Although I believe putting yourself on five or more online dating sites is a bit overboard, some do see this as an efficient way of finding their match.

Many online dating sites tend to keep their proprietary algorithms closely guarded. However, some of the larger companies tend to use algorithms based on information provided by users. Therefore, when responding to dating sites questions; be honest. This way, you have a higher chance of getting matches that best meet your interest.

Putting your trust in dating sites use of algorithms may help you find your potential partner, but it should not be the only method. As indicated earlier, I recommend that you develop a list of what you desire in a mate and refer to it as you search for a potential compatible partner on dating sites. Your chances of finding your match are just as good, if not better, than the algorithms that many dating sites use to help you find your match.

In a way, your needs list in its purest form is an ideal method of identifying your match. Many of the factors you are using are similar factors that dating sites also use. What is different is that you are personalizing it to your specifications and personal needs. Now, assuming that you have identified your uncompromising and compromising needs as indicated in Chapter 2, the next step is to use that vital information to quantify those needs on a point factor chart.

I call it, a Compatibility Point Factor Chart. It consists of a table that includes many factors that you value or desire in a mate. It's a tool to help you find your compatible partner. The Chart is user-friendly if built on an Excel spreadsheet or something similar. The point and percentage calculations are automatically done for you on the worksheet. Let me breakdown the Chart into its parts. Depending on your particular needs and desires, your Chart listing may vary or be similar to others. That's the great thing about the Chart; it's largely tailor-made to your specifications. As a result of the Chart customization with your needs, it helps to validation if a person you see on a dating site is a potentially good match for you. The Chart can also be used for potential partner's you meet even offline, such as people you come in contact at parties, bars, religious events, reunions, and other special events.

Age Range Factor

Most if not all, dating sites use age as among its factors in categorizing its members. It's one of the main features online member use when search for a match. It's only practical that serious online dating seekers that are looking for long-term relationships search for someone in their age range. Besides, most want someone they can relate to not only intellectually but also generationally. Although like many things in relationships, there are exceptions where couples are at significant differences in age have had very successful long-term relationships. Not only does this include where the man is over ten years older than the woman, but also where the woman is more than ten years older than the man.

Another thing that should be noted about age is that we have more than one type of age. When we talk about age, most of us are referring to our chronological age. However, there is also our physical and mental or psychological age, which is not always aligned with our chronological age. For example, a person can be chronologically age 55, but physically look and feel like age 45, and mentally act as though they are age 35. This can also apply when one can be age 40 but look like they are physically age 50 and act like they are age 65.

So, when considering a compatible mate, don't only judge them by their chronological age; take into consideration also their physical and mental age as well. It can be argued that the physical and mental or psychological age factors are more important than the chronological age factor. However, for the sake of the age range factor on the Compatibility Point Factor Chart, we will focus on the chronological age. The physical and mental age factor can indirectly be weighed in other parts of the Chart, which we will get into shortly.

To show how the Chart works, let's take, for example, a single 45-year-old black female living in Chicago. We will call her Debra

Owens. Ms. Owens is a sales manager for a conservative radio station. The factors on her Chart would be used for all potential matches she finds on a dating site that appeals to her. Individually we will go over the design of each section of the Chart and later show how it can be completed for those potential partners she finds on dating sites.

On the age section of the Chart Ms. Owens would first fill in the age range, starting with the ideal age range she would like in a partner. Next, she would complete the second age range she would consider, and so forth, listing four age range fields. The ranges in age can be as short or long as desired. The only set items on the age range factor are that the point's distribution is a 20 points difference, as listed in the example below. Returning to our case with Ms. Owens, she wants to target men in the age range of 42 to 52. This is her ideal chronological age range; therefore, this range will have the highest points (100) she can obtain for this factor. However, if she finds someone on a dating site that she is attracted to and possibly a good match that is age 54; Ms. Owens include 80 points for that particular person since it's not her ideal age range that she prefers. The points she selected for this factor would be later multiplied by 10 percent.

Age Range	Pts.	Pts. Total
42 - 52	100	
53 - 57	80	
37 - 41	60	
31 - 36	40	
(Selected Pts x 10%)		0

Height Factor

Women and men generally are particular about the height of their partner. Women usually prefer that their partner be taller than they and men prefer that their partner be shorter than them. Therefore, height is a legitimate factor that both women and men take into consideration when searching online for a potential mate.

In Ms. Owens case, she selected the height range of 5.10 to 6.3 as her preference. Therefore, this height range would have 100 points and would be multiplied by 5 percent.

Height	Pts.	Pts. Total
5.10 - 6.3	**100**	
6.4 - 6.7	80	
5.8 - 5.9	60	

(Selected Pts x 5%)	**0**

Weight Factor

Like one's height, one's weight can play an acceptance or rejection role for women and men seeking a mate. Many people are open to dating those that are a little overweight, but it is those that people find extremely over or underweight that ends up getting ignored by users searching for a mate. However, there are many attractive, appealing, and likable people on dating sites that have weight issues. Some may be able to control their overweight problems while others may be unable to because of medical issues or poor eating habits.

Overlooking potential partners because of their weight issues may be unwise. Such persons may still meet many of your other significant needs. But again, everyone has their likes and dislikes. However, if you prefer a particular size in a partner, complete the weight factor accordingly.

You will also find some people on dating sites that are self-conscious about their weight and may not show full-body photos of themselves. Regardless of their weight concerns, if you still have an interest in such a person, it may be better to avoid talking about their weight until you had a chance to get to know them better. Women generally seem to be more self-conscious about their weight than men; therefore, men should be cautious when asking a woman about their weight or body in general when they are not showing a full-body photo of themselves in their profile photos. The best approach is to bring the subject up after you both had a few conversations and have shown mutual interest in each other.

Ms. Owens, in our example, prefer someone of average or athletic size; therefore she would list 100 points for that weight/size factor as listed below and those points would be multiplied by 5 percent.

Weight/Size	Pts.	Pts. Total
Average Weight/Athletic	**100**	
Under Weight/Thin	80	
Thick Weight/Voluptuous	60	
Over Weight/Fat	40	
(Selected Pts x 5%)		0

Mileage Factor

Many people consciously take into consideration how far one lives from them when they search for compatible partners on online dating sites. For many, the longer the distance someone is from them, the less likely are they willing to consider them a legitimate potential match. During the dating process, couples want the assurance that their mate is accessible to them when needed, and it would not take them over an hour or so to get to their location.

Of course, there are exceptions. Others are more open to dating someone long distance, mainly if they are heads over hills about each other and don't mind putting in the growing miles on their car. But, traveling back and forth over 100 miles can become somewhat stressful, especially during winter time or other times when the weather is poor for driving conditions.

But again, the majority of people on dating sites prefer that their match is within close driving distance. So, mileage is a valid factor people take into consideration when reviewing dating sites profiles.

In our example of Ms. Owens, she shows that she would prefer someone that is no more than 20 miles away. Therefore, her first preference in terms of distance of a compatible mate is that he lives no farther than 20 miles or less. The mileage factor would equate to 100 points. The points would be multiplied by 15 percent.

Mileage (one way)	Pts.	Pts. Total
Up to 20 miles	**100**	
Up to 40 miles	80	
Up to 60 miles	60	
Up to 80 miles	40	
Up to 100 miles	20	
Over 100 miles (Long Dist)	0	
(Selected Pts x 15%)		0

Housing Situation Factor

I talked with several people about this particular factor. For some, it is not considered a concern; for others, it is. When we refer to the housing situation, we are addressing who lives with the person of interest. Does that person live with pets, children, or their parents?

Not everyone likes pets; some are downright allergic to certain kinds of animals. Also, many, primarily middle-aged and older adults, whether they admit it or not, prefer that their dates not have young children which can sometimes make dating an inconvenience. Also, adult children living in the house can create uncomfortable situations when a couple is trying to have privacy. So, consciously or unconsciously, people do weigh the housing situations of their potential partner.

In the example below, Ms. Owens prefers that her potential match lives alone and therefore would include 100 points for that preference. Note that she has listed 80 points for at least three other items on the list. This is acceptable only if Ms. Owens feels equally the same about them. However, if she felt different about the other three categories, there would be a 20 points difference between each. For this particular factor, you can give the same amount of points if it applies similarly to how you feel about that living situation. This factor would be multiplied by 5 percent.

Housing Situation	Pts.	Pts. Total
Lives Alone	**100**	
Lives with Children	80	
Lives with Children and/or Pets	80	
Lives with Pets	80	
Lives with Roommate	60	
Lives with More than 1 Roommate	40	
(Selected Pts x 5%)		0

Political Affiliation Factor

Some people are more passionate about politics than others and put a high premium on their political affiliation. They would not think of considering a mate that does not share their same political values. It is for this reason such a factor is worth considering.

Surveys have shown that couples that share same or similar political values tend to have more successful relationships. But again, like other factors we have discussed, there are exceptions. However, if your partner viewpoints are in constant conflict with your own on such topics as the economy, war, or other sensitive issues, it could spill over into the stability of the relationship itself.

Many times when dating couples discover that their political views and values do not align, they find themselves in polarized arguments. However, with all things in loving relationships, couples with different political views should learn to compromise or respect the other's viewpoint. This, of course, does not mean you have to abandon your political opinions but agree to disagree. If couples allow politics to destroy a relationship, then one has to question whether that relationship was strong anyway. But, if you want to avoid such political conflict, then seeking a partner with similar political views may be the direction to go.

In our example with Ms. Owens, she is a conservative Republican. Therefore she assigned 100 points for both the Republican and Conservative factor as listed below. As with the housing situation factor, this is among the factors which can be assigned the same amount of points if the person feels the same way about one or more political affiliations. Note that this factor points would be multiplied by 5 percent.

Political Affiliation	Pts.	Pts. Total
Republican	**100**	
Conservative	**100**	
Independent	80	
None Political	60	
Democrat	40	
Liberal	20	
(Selected Pts x 5%)		0

Physical Attraction Factor

Physical attraction does not have to be something that you are born with; it can also be gain through other ways through the cosmetic procedure and other methods. However, physical attraction can be subjective. Beauty is always in the eyes of the beholder. But certain people have magnified beauty that appeals to the masses. For example, most people will find actress Halle Berry more attractive than actress Whoopi Goldberg. So, certain forms of physical attraction can be arguably universal.

As mentioned in the first chapter, it is one's physical attraction that is the first thing that captures our attention whether we see them in person or online. We almost instinctively become attracted to that person's appearance whether or not they are a good match for us or not. So, ignoring physical attraction would be fooling ourselves when we search dating sites for a compatible mate. Therefore, it is one of the factors that should be included in the Compatibility Point Factor Chart. But, after we come to know that person that we are physically attracted to, the appeal could increase or wane at some degree.

Below is how the point's distribution would look for physical attraction on the Compatibility Point Factor Chart for Ms. Owens. Unlike the housing situation and political affiliation factors which the same amount of points can be given (with some limitations), for the physical attraction factor, points assigned should be separated by 20 points each. This factor points would be multiplied by 5 percent.

Physical Attraction	Pts.	Pts. Total
Very Attractive	**100**	
Attractive	80	
Average	60	
Below Average	40	

(Selected Pts x 5%)		0

Uncompromising Needs Factor

As mentioned in the previous two chapters, your most essential needs are your uncompromising needs. These are considered your deal-breakers in your efforts to find your long-term partner. Because of their fundamental importance to you, they will represent the highest percentage of your points. Some of the most common uncompromising needs are honesty, commitment, trustworthy, non-smoker, non-drug user, financially stable, faithfulness, and so forth.

However, as people change through the years, their uncompromising needs can also change. This can be due to lifestyle changes, maturity, and other situations in which values may change. So, some of your uncompromising needs may later in your relationships become compromising needs, or no longer a need at all. For example, what was an uncompromising need during your 40s may not be an unyielding need during your 50s or 60s.

So, as we indicated in Chapter 2, know what needs you must have in a relationship. Be true to yourself by making sure you accurately identify what values or needs that are most important to you and will not compromise. As indicated earlier, you want to list your uncompromising needs and transfer them to the uncompromising needs factor on the Chart. But they must be limited to five elements. The whole concept of the uncompromising needs list is to not only help you identify what's most important to you in a relationship, but also identify those potential partners that are most compatible with you.

Returning to our Ms. Owens example, her uncompromising needs would be the following. Note for her uncompromising needs she has a maximum of five choices, and the points for each would be totaled together. If she wanted to make any of those needs less than five, that would be fine, but she must be aware that it would decrease her point totals. Also, note for this category all the needs equate to 150 points each, and the totaled points would be multiplied by 30 percent.

Uncompromising Needs	Pts.	Pts. Total
Honesty	150	
Thoughtfulness	150	
Trustworthy	150	
Committed to Serious Relation	150	
Good Communicator	150	
(Total Selected Pts x 30%)		0

Compromising Needs Factor

Finally, there are the non-deal-breakers, the compromising needs. Sometimes what we thought was a deal-breaker for us was not really one at all. For example, if you are a religious person and believe strongly that your partner must also be religious but find a potential partner that meets most of your uncompromising needs except being religious; then you might be willing to remove that item from your deal-breaker list and place on your non-deal-breaker list. Because compromising needs are not as crucial of a necessity as uncompromising needs, you would give 75 points for each of these types of desires. Also, like the uncompromising needs, you have a maximum of five kinds of needs to list for your compromising needs. However, just as with your uncompromising needs, you can list less than five, but again this will shorten your point totals. Below is an example of Ms. Owens compromising needs. The total points for this factor would be multiplied by 20 percent.

Compromising Needs	Pts.	Pts. Total
Believes in God	75	
Religious	75	
Attends Church	75	
Romantic	75	
Goal Oriented	75	
(Total Selected Pts x 20%)		0

Completing the Compatibility Point Factor Chart

Now that you have an idea of how to make up a Compatibility Point Factor Chart, it's time to fill in the point totals using the example we have been working with for Debra Owens. Below is her completed Chart. Remember, your Chart may be different, based upon your specific needs in a long-term relationship. Ms. Owens need choices are highlighted along with the points and total. She may utilize this Chart (preferably on an Excel spreadsheet) for all the men she finds on online dating sites that are desirable, interesting, but more importantly, compatible to her values, character, and overall needs.

Of course, as mentioned before, the use of the Chart does not have to be limited to online dating sites, it can also be used on potential partners you meet offline such as at parties, reunions, business affairs, and other events where the opposite sex meet and mingle.

The factors you selected with the highest points are both tied to your values, needs, and desires. They also reflect what you are looking for in a long-term relationship. But suppose you are not looking for a long-term relationship. For example, you may be just looking for someone to hang out with or share hobbies. Or maybe you are gay and want to use the Chart to find a match in a same-sex relationship. The Chart may still be used for such types of relationships. But it's primarily designed for heterosexual men and women seeking long-term relationships.

Below, we will review Debra Owens completed Chart. Let's look at her point totals for a potential match she found on a popular online dating site and what it all means.

Age Range	Pts.PT	Height	Pts.	PT	Weight/Size	Pts.PT	PS
42 - 52	100 **100**	5.10 - 6.3	100	**100**	Average Weight/Athletic	100 **100**	
53 - 57	80	6.4 - 6.7	80		Under Weight/Thin	80	
37 - 41	60	5.8 - 5.9	60		Thick Weight/Voluptuous	60	
31 - 36	40				Over Weight/Fat	40	

(Selected Pts x 10%)	10	(Selected Pts x 5%)	5	(Selected Pts x 5%)	5	20

Mileage (one way)	Pts.PT	Housing Situation	Pts.	PT	Political Affiliation	Pts.PT
Up to 20 miles	100 **100**	Lives Alone	100	**100**	Republican	100 **100**
Up to 40 miles	80	Lives with Children	80		Conservative	100
Up to 60 miles	60	Lives w/ Children and/or Pets	80		Independent	80
Up to 80 miles	40	Lives with Pets	80		Non-Political	60
Up to 100 miles	20	Lives with Roommate	60		Democrat	40
Over 100 miles (LD)	0	Lives w/ More than 1 Roommate	40		Liberal	20

(Selected Pts x 15%)	15	(Selected Pts x 5%)	5	(Selected Pts x 5%)	5	25

Physical Attraction	Pts.PT	Uncompromising Needs	Pts.	PT	Compromising Needs	Pts.PT
Very Attractive	100 **100**	Sense of Humor	150	**150**	Great Cook	75 **75**
Attractive	80	Christian	150	**150**	Enjoys Music	75 **75**
Average	60	Faithful	150	**150**	Thoughtful	75 **75**
Below Average	40	Committed to Serious Relation	150	**150**	Dress Well	75 **75**
		Good Communicator	150	**150**	Likes Sex	75 **75**

(Selected Pts x 5%)	5	(Total Selected Pts x 30%)	225	(Total Selected Pts x 20%)	75	305

350 pts = Highest Pts Obtainable   350

Number of points short of highest pts..=   0

Name   SoulSearcher910

Review of the Sample Chart

Forty-five-year-old Debra Owens, who is single and lives in Chicago, has listed on the Age Range Factor section of the Chart that 42 to 52 is her age range preference. Therefore, anyone, Ms. Owens finds on dating sites that appeal to her, and she believes may be a good match at this age range would get 100 points. If Ms. Owens, however, finds someone in an optional second choice age range, such as 53 to 57, that she considers interesting and compatible, then Ms. Owens would give that person with the alternative age range 80 points. All points are entered next to the right of the corresponding points she selected and multiplied by a specific percentage, as shown at the bottom of the section for each factor on the Chart. For example, the 100 points Debra Owens gave for age range 42 to 52 is multiplied by 10% resulting in 10 points (in a square box) for the Age Range Factor.

The other factors (Height, Weight/Size, and Mileage) are completed in the same concept. For Housing Situation and Political Affiliation Factors, note that, as Ms. Owens has done, you can give the same number of points if you feel the same way for Republican and Conservative. However, you can only use one of those selections for your actual point total as shown in the examples for Housing Situation and Political Affiliation.

For the factors under Physical Attraction, there should be 20 points differences, like that for Age Range, Height, Weight/Size, and Mileage Factors.

As shown in the example, the numbering arrangement gets a little different for Uncompromising and Compromising Needs factors. For both these sections, you can list a maximum of five factors, and you can count each point for those five factors. However, you also have the option of limiting to less than five. But be aware, that would lessen the number of total points you would have acquired on the Chart for a perspective partner. But, it's feasible that you don't have five uncompromising or compromising needs and you should apply that accordingly on your Chart. Note also that your uncompromising needs are multiplied by 30 percent because of their level of importance to you; and your compromising needs are multiplied by 20 percent because of their second level of importance in finding a compatible mate that aligns with your values, interests, and character. So, together, these two critical categories represent 50 percent of your point totals.

Below the Chart list is Ms. Owens completed point-factor evaluation for a prospective partner with the username "SoulSearcher910." He received 350 points as a result of Ms. Owens point-factor evaluation of him. As shown, this is the highest points obtainable on the Chart and indicates that SoulSearcher910 potentially is a strong match. This, of course, demonstrates to Ms. Owens that SoulSearcher910 would be worth pursuing or getting to know better. But keep in mind, the Chart, to some extent, can be subjective. Many of the factors she listed under uncompromising and compromising needs are usually not listed or confirmed on SoulSearcher910 online dating profile. Ms. Owens must get confirmation on the needs which she ranked him on. The same process would be for anyone else. Yes, a person on their profile may say they are honest, trustworthy, and kind, but communicating and going out with that person will be the determining factor that confirms or validate those factors being true. So, keep in mind, the Compatibility Point Factor Chart is a tool to help you identify your potential mate; you still need to get confirmation on their actual compatibility to you.

The Compatibility Chart Key and Meaning

Pts Range			Compatibility Levels	PS
350	to	335	Strong Match	15
334	to	304	Good Match	30
303	to	258	Satisfactory Match	45
257	to	0	Poor Match	

Above is the key to the sum of points obtainable in evaluating the total points on your Compatibility Point Factor Chart. Total points ranging from 350 to 335 equate to a Strong Match. Total points ranging from 334 to 304 relate to a Good Match. Anyone that falls into these two match groups is worth taking seriously as a potential match. Those with points ranging from 303 to 258 equate to a Satisfactory Match. The people that fall into this group are obviously not as strong of a potential match, but some may be long-shots and possibly worth some consideration. Anyone with total points at 257 or below would be a Poor Match. Don't waste your time considering these people as a potential match. The column PS (point spread) shows the point spread of the ranges. For example, the point spread for Strong Match is 15 points.

Again, it's best to complete your Chart on an Excel spreadsheet or something equivalent that allows you to use formulas that will quickly calculate points and percentages for you. Your Chart would be different from others because it is made of characteristics, values, and needs you personally desire in a relationship. You want to utilize the Chart for only those you seemed compatible to, attracted to, or have similar values. There is no need to waste time in completing a chart on someone that you have no interest in or do not share anything in common. The ultimate purpose of the Compatibility Point Factor Chart is to help you find your potential match and move forward to the communicating process to get to know that person better and determine the level or degree that you are a strong or good match.

Many, if not most of the answers to your questions on whether a person measures up to your uncompromising and compromising needs would require some communications with that person because again it would probably not be indicated in their profile. For example, they may say they are thoughtful and considerate, but the truth can only be exposed through actual communication and observation with that person.

Relying on your gut feeling about someone is not enough when it comes to searching for your potential match on online dating sites. The Compatibility Point Factor Chart is a tool that helps you more successful in identifying someone that shares your values and interests.

The following Chart completion example belongs to a 60-year-old white male. It gives perspective on how one may complete a chart differently. We will call the person in our example, Fred Winston.

Age Range	Pts.PT	Height	Pts.	PT	Weight/Size	Pts.PT PS
53 - 63	100 **100**	5.1 - 5.3	100		Average Weight/Athletic	100 **100**
52 - 49	80	5.4 - 5.7	80	80	Under Weight/Thin	80
64 - 67	60	5.8 - 5.10	60		Thick Weight/Voluptuous	60
48 - 46	40				Over Weight/Fat	40

(Selected Pts x 10%) **10** | (Selected Pts x 5%) **4** | (Selected Pts x 5%) **5** 19

Mileage (one way)	Pts.PT	Housing Situation	Pts.	PT	Political Affiliation	Pts.PT
Up to 20 miles	100	Lives with Pets	100	**100**	None Political	100
Up to 40 miles	80 **80**	Lives with Children	80		Independent	80
Up to 60 miles	60	Lives w/ Children and/or Pets	80		Conservative	60
Up to 80 miles	40	Lives Alone	80		Republican	60 **60**
Up to 100 miles	20	Lives with Roommate	60		Democrat	40
Over 100 miles (LD)	0	Lives w/ More than 1 Roommate	40		Liberal	20

(Selected Pts x 15%) **12** | (Selected Pts x 5%) **5** | (Selected Pts x 5%) **3** 20

Physical Attraction	Pts.PT	Uncompromising Needs	Pts.	PT	Compromising Needs	Pts.PT
Very Attractive	100	Sense of Humor	150	**150**	Great Cook	75
Attractive	80 **80**	Christian	150		Enjoys Music	75 **75**
Average	60	Faithful	150	**150**	Thoughtful	75 **75**
Below Average	40	Committed to Serious Relation	150	**150**	Dress Well	75 **75**
		Good Communicator	150	**150**	Likes Sex	75 **75**

(Selected Pts x 5%) **4** | (Total Selected Pts x 30%) **180** | (Total Selected Pts x 20%) **60** 244

350 pts = Highest Pts Obtainable **283**

Number of points short of highest pts..=   67

Name WonderfulGirl391

The Compatibility Point Factor Chart completed by Mr. Winston on a potential match he saw online with the username WonderfulGirl391, gives some insight on how a male may complete the Chart. Note that the woman was not a Christian. This was one of Mr. Winston's uncompromising needs; therefore, he could not give her the 150 points for that factor. Because of the number of points not credited for having that factor along with some other lower points, her points total was limited to 283. Based upon the key below, WonderfulGirl391 would be a Satisfactory Match, but not as strong of a possible match for him at the other two top levels. Because of the lesser number of points obtained from the Chart, WonderfulGirl391 would not be a strong or good match for Mr. Winston.

Compatibility Chart Key

Pts Range			Compatibility Levels	PS
350	to	335	Strong Match	15
334	to	304	Good Match	30
303	to	258	Satisfactory Match	45
257	to	0	Poor Match	

Not only do you now have a tool to measure the compatibility of potential matches on online dating sites, but you can also use this same Chart (particularly the uncompromising and compromising factors) to help write your profile for online dating sites that you may join. Specific elements in these two sections can be referred to when you list information about your character, values, and interests.

Key Points to Remember or Act Upon

- A Compatibility Point Factor Chart consists of a table that includes many factors that you value or desire in a mate. It's a tool used to help you find your compatible partner.
- The Compatibility Point Factor Chart helps you weigh or measure the fit potential of those you may be interested in on dating sites. You can also use the Chart to help write your online profile.
- As men and women change through the years, their uncompromising needs can also change. This can be due to lifestyle changes, maturity, and other situations in which values may change.
- Relying on your gut feeling about someone is not enough when it comes to searching for your potential match on online dating sites. The Compatibility Point Factor Chart is a tool that helps you to be more successful in identifying someone that shares your values.
- It's best to complete your Chart on an Excel spreadsheet or something equivalent that allows you to use formulas that will quickly calculate points and percentage totals.

Chapter 4

Selecting the Best Dating Sites for Long-Term Relationships

The best online dating sites for you may not necessarily be the best for someone else. First realize that all types of people appear on various dating sites, even those sites not necessarily geared for their needs. Some online dating sites are larger than others, and some are free while the majority requires a paid subscription for the full use of its sites. To determine what online dating site would be in your best interest in selecting a long-term relationship, visit the dating sites, and review the available information on those sites. Also, take a look at independent reviews on these sites that can be found on the Internet and read what they say about them. Also, as part of your decision, determine whether you want to join a free site or a paid site. Many free sites also have paid subscriptions as an upgrade to their free subscription. So, knowing the demographics of online dating sites, their size, and costs is an excellent start to figuring out which dating sites are best for your needs.

When reading the information on dating websites, carefully read the fine print. Also, view details on how the sites are operated, types of features they have, and other information that helps you to decide what dating sites meet your specific relationship search needs.

While viewing the variety of online dating sites take notes and compare the information with other sites. Evaluate each feature side-by-side on an Excel spreadsheet or something equivalent to determine how they measure up against each other. You don't have to shop for an online dating site like you would for a new car, but you should put some time and effort into seeking out the best dating websites. Doing so will enhance your chances of finding a long term partner in the most efficient manner.

Also, as a starting point, begin your search with those online dating sites that already have a good track record of catering to singles and divorced people seeking long-term relationships. Again, search the Internet and other resources which provide independent information on such things as statistics on which sites members have a more significant percentage of marriages.

Independent reviewers and surveys are found plentiful on the Internet. For example, there are online survey data on dating sites in general from Static Brain, Statista, Pew Research, and Online Dating Magazine. Independent statistical information on dating sites can be utilized as a barometer for judging not only dating sites long-term match-making success rate, but also other statistical data as well.

Some Dating Sites with Successful Track Record on Long-Term Relationships

With there being over 2,500 dating sites in the U.S in 2019, and more than 1,000 new online dating sites created almost annually, singles have plenty of options where to search for love online. But which dating sites among this ever-growing dating market does the best job of hooking up singles seeking long-term relationships? Well, surveys and statistics from those surveys can vary; depending on how they were conducted, who took the survey, and what kinds of questions were asked in the study. However, one of the best ways to evaluate survey data is to review more than one source of data. If more than two or more independent sources of survey data are similar or consistent, then such data may have more validating value.

Based on the consistent data I have seen from year to year, Match.com, eHarmony, and Plenty of Fish (POF) seem to have a good track record for successful long-term relationships. However, this does not mean other online dating sites fall short in hooking singles up for long-term relationships. Many others also do a great job, but these three dating sites seem to be consistent leaders in helping singles find long-term partners, including those that marry. They also do a rather good job in marketing their success rate in matching singles for long-term relationships. However, things change quickly in the online dating world. Those dating sites that are among the top for more serious relationships today may be replaced by others tomorrow. Also, rankings tend to differ among the various reviewers and surveyors of online dating sites. Therefore, it is recommended to take everyone's ranking of dating sites, including mine, with a grain of salt.

Here is a summary of the three top dating sites, I believe, has consistently done a great job of helping singles find long-term relationships. Note that most of the information on these online dating sites are as of 2018 and 2019; some may have changed as of this publication date (2019). Visit the individual websites for membership rates and other related information.

Match.com

Match.com has been the most successful of dating sites in the U.S., and as of this writing, it continues to rank at the top or among the best five online dating sites. Match.com is not prosperous because it was the first online dating site in the U.S. created in 1995; it's successful because of its large membership; ability to attract new members; and maintain a database of compatible members that are pleased with its services. Other dating sites are also successful at this, but Match.com is the leader and usually appears at the top of annual survey lists of pinnacle dating sites.

According to the site, it allows various free writing sections for its members to express themselves. Members also can post up to 26 photos and selected preferences on the person they are seeking. Like many other reputable dating sites, members profile and photos are screened to ensure the integrity of its community members.

The online dating site boasts that it's the top site for online dating and its members have more dates, relationships, and marriages than any other dating sites. It would be difficult to argue with such claim given its favorable statistics, longevity, and membership size.

Speaking of statistics, as of October 2018, Match.com percentage of users were: 39 percent Generation X (between ages 39-53 as of 2018); 32 percent Millennials (between ages 24-38 as of 2018); and 27 percent Baby Boomers (between ages 54-74 as of 2018). Also, according to the site, it has created 10 million relationships as of that period. It would be safe to say that all of these percentages may have increased in 2019 and potentially do so in 2020 and beyond.

eHarmony

eHarmony, launched in 2000, was the first algorithm-based dating site. When you speak of dating sites with a reputation for matching people searching for long-term relationships, eHarmony is the gold standard among online dating sites. It is geared toward those that are only serious of looking for long-term relationships. If you are looking for a fling, one-night stand, or any other casual type relationship, eHarmony is not the dating site for you.

With its detailed profiles, members' information includes their likes and dislikes, what they consider their best life skills, how they spend their leisure time, how their friends would describe them, and more. Such type of profiles data surely gives you more in-depth information about prospective partners, which better help you evaluate their compatibility with you.

The company does an excellent job of suggesting matches based upon your personality survey and profile settings. Historically, the average age of eHarmony users has been in the mid-30 range. Like many other online dating websites, users increase during the holidays through Valentine's Day.

The dating site has been very successful in promoting its focus on long-term relationships. For example, it has advertised that it has been responsible for 5 percent of all U.S. marriages. Of course, proving such a statement would require some complex research and tricky math.

In 2017, eHarmony allowed users to see why they were considered compatible with a potential partner with a feature known as "The Two of You Together." It also allowed users to see the matches who scored at an advanced level of compatibility and the reason why.

The dating sit runs a tight ship and does not accept just anyone. For example, it boasts that since it launched its dating sites in 2000, it had rejected about a million people that applied to use its services. According to the site, about 30 percent of those applicants were denied because they were discovered already married. Also, about 27 percent were rejected because they were younger than the minimum application age of 21. Another 9 percent were declined because they provided inconsistent responses to their application. Therefore, if you are considering joining eHarmony, make sure you're not already married, you're at least age 21 or older, and you are consistent and honest in responding to their application questions.

I'm sure eHarmony members appreciate the match-making dating site's gate-keeping vigilance.

Plenty of Fish

I must admit that I was surprised by reports that Plenty of Fish was among the top sites for long-term relationships. I have seen others reporting that its best for those seeking casual dating relationships. However, there have been many people who have been successful in long-term relationships as a result of meeting on this site. Several of these people have also gotten married. Therefore, arguably, this site should be seriously considered among the top dating sites for long-term relationships.

Plenty of Fish, launched in 2003, has been around for a while. Big credit to its appeal is that it's free to use, including communicating with other users, both paid and unpaid users. The site periodically promotes its upgrade services to unpaid members.

As of 2019, Plenty of Fish claims it has 3 million active users and is the largest dating site.

According to a 2014 report, 85 percent of the site users log in via mobile devices. That percentage most likely has increased since that time period. In 2016, Plenty of Fish stated that 20 percent of its users ranged in ages 18 to 24; 38 percent ranged in ages 25 to 34; 22 percent ranged in ages 35 to 44, and 20 percent ranged in ages 45 or older. Today there is likely a slight difference in these percentages and ranges but probably not significantly.

The site also has a personality test that helps to provide improved matches. It also has an advanced search function that allows you to search for compatible matches based on factors such as pets, religion, education, and even hair and eye color. For serious users, the advanced search function can be a helpful tool in finding your long-term match because you have a variety of useful factors to assist in your search.

Don't expect to get a lot of information from many of Plenty of Fish members essay section. Despite the site giving users a large amount of space to write information about themselves, many users write only a few sentences. Some may simply say "Just Ask" or something similar. However, there are a significant number of serious users that provide sufficient information about themselves that inspire readers' interest and motivate them to respond to their profiles.

Because Plenty of Fish is free, one has to be aware that scammers also appear on the site. This, of course, is common to other free online dating services. Such scammers would post a fake profile aimed at both male and female users in the hope of scamming them out of money or stealing their identity.

Plenty of Fish, as with other free dating sites don't only make money from their upgrade members, but also make money from ads. Also, Plenty of Fish and many other dating sites, both free and paid may sell some of your information to marketers and different related types of organizations. Such use of your data can be found in terms of agreement statement by Plenty of Fish as well as other dating sites agreement statements.

Other Top Dating Sites for Serious Relationships

EliteSingles is among those dating sites that are also best suited for singles looking for a serious or long-term relationship. It seems to have a lengthy signup process that includes a thorough questionnaire. I'm sure it has to do with its ability to provide its users with quality matches for potential long-term relationships. The site also has some fraud protection measures in place to ensure your online dating experience is secured. EliteSingles also promotes itself as the dating site for educated professionals looking for long-term and serious relationships. It boasts about 67 percent of all its members have a college degree.

OurTime has to be considered as a dating site with an objective of matching singles for serious relationships. The dating site is dedicated to mature singles over age 50. The site does provide free membership that includes registering, browsing, and flirting. More features are available when you upgrade to a paid membership. For OurTime basic search, the filters include gender, location, and relationship type. For the advanced search, you have more detail preferences, including interests, education background, appearance, religion, and other choices. When the site finds someone compatible with you via its algorithm, it informs you in its matches section. According to one review, about 8.9 million people visit the site monthly.

With there being more than 2,500 dating sites in the U.S., there are several dating sites that are a good fit for those looking for serious or long-term relationships. Some I must admit I never heard of before. But among those that I am familiar with that are worth mentioning include **ChristianMingle, BlackPeopleMeet, OkCupid**, and **Tinder**. All of these particular dating sites also offer free trials.

The bottom line is that you can also find singles seeking long-term relationships on many dating sites known for casual dating. Your job would be to seek out those people that are looking for such type of relationship and are compatible with you.

Key Points to Remember or Act Upon

- To determine what online dating site would be in your best interest in a long-term relationship, visit, and review the available information about them. Also, read independent reviews about dating sites that interest you.
- When reading the information on dating websites, carefully read the fine print. Also, learn how it's operated, types of features it has, and other information that will help you to decide if it meets your long-term relationship search needs.
- Independent reviewers and surveys on dating sites can be found all over the Internet. Past survey data can be found from organizations such as Static Brain, Statista, Pew Research, and Online Dating Magazine.

Chapter 5

Ways to Post Profiles that Attract Your Potential Match

If you are "fishing" for a long-term partner, it's only appropriate that you use proper bait. One that will attract the attention of the specific type of partner you're seeking regardless of the other lures that have the potential of distracting their attention in different directions. By-the-way, your profile is your bait. It must grab the attention of those you are seeking. Therefore, your profile photos must be captivating and appealing to the eyes; and the written portion of your profile should easily reflect your real personality and other traits. In a nutshell, you want to be genuine and stand out from the crowd of other profiles. But you also want to make sure your profile is attracting the type of potential partner you desire. Although you may attract others that are not a good fit for you, your goal is to find users that are potentially a compatible match for you.

Go on any online dating sites, and you will surely see some poorly taken photos. Make sure your photos are not among these badly taken pictures. Unpleasant photos have a negative reflection on your profile.

Some of the written portions of profiles will also be weak among the many you see on dating sites. Some people hardly say anything in their profiles, leaving one to wonder can they write.

If you are serious about finding your match, you must be willing to put in some decent effort in writing and posting a profile with some wow factor. Some of the information on your Compatibility Point Factor Chart will help you generate ideas for what you may want to include in writing your profile. You may want to make a written draft of what you want to say in your profile. But before focusing on the written portion of your profile, let's start with the photos first. It is the photos that will be the initial attention grabber on your profile.

Posting Photos that Captivates the Viewer Eyes

Think variety, clarity, lighting, focus, and personality when preparing and posting photos on your online dating profile. Even how you post a photo on your profile can be a reflection of how you are perceived. A picture with poor lighting and out of focus issues says that you didn't care how you looked online or you took little effort in posting how others would see you. So, take the initiative of making sure that the photos you post on your profile are of good quality. Also, you don't have to be or hire a professional photographer to do this. Nor will you need a fancy or expensive camera for taking good quality photos. Today's Smartphone's, androids, and, of course, consumer cameras take excellent photos provided you take them correctly.

Whether you take the photo yourself or have someone else take pictures of you, make sure the shots are not blurry, dark, grainy, or out of focus. Proper lighting is one of the primary keys of good quality photos. Although particular environment conditions may limit the amount of light available to you at the time your pictures are taken. Consider having your main profile photo taken in a controlled environment where you can manipulate and control the lighting. Also, avoid posting any of those selfies pictures in which people can see you in the photo holding a Smartphone toward a mirror as you take pictures of yourself. These types of images seem to not come off well in terms of style. Taking photographs of yourself posing while holding up a Smartphone in your hand gives your photos a tacky look. If you can edit out the appearance of the Smartphone in your hand; it would help improve such images. Another option with a cell phone is to prop up the phone, such as against a book or other object. Put the phone in video mold and videotape yourself. Next select a clear still frame from the video and post to your profile page. Another option is to have someone to either take photos of you or borrow a relative or friend's camera that has a timer that allows you to take pictures of yourself.

The number of photos you post on your profile is up to you and the limitations that dating sites allow. However, you may want to include at least three to five photos, therefore, allowing you to show a variety of types of images that reflect you and your personality. Try also to include pictures of you in different environments that reveal something about you and your interest. For example, such photos can be of you in the park, at a family or class reunion, or any other event where the environment is different. By all means, don't post all photo shots of you taken at home or one other single site, unless of course, you're only posting one or two photos.

Your main photo, the one that viewers first see of you, should be at least somewhat current. This should be your best photo. It should also be a well-lighted headshot of you smiling. And make sure this main photo does not cover up your eyes with sunglasses. People want to see your eyes, especially in your main profile photo. If you regularly wear eyeglasses, make sure the picture does not reflect glare from your glasses. Also, include one or more candid photos of you engaged in some activities such as playing tennis, dancing, or some other activities or events that reflect your hobbies or interests. Such type of photos adds balance to your posted photos. Many people also find candid online images more interesting than posed photos. Although the majority of your photos should show you smiling, consider throwing in at least one or two pictures of you not smiling, but not necessarily frowning. Maybe include a photo of you blowing a playful kiss or one of you in deep thought. The key is to add variety in the images that you post on your profile page. Also, consider at least one photo of you slightly dressed up. For example, men may want to include at least one photo in a suit and tie and for women, at least one photo in a dress outfit. Pictures of this kind give people an idea of how you look when going out to an event or former affair. Also, date your photos; you need not provide an exact date, simply type under the photo the month and year it was taken, or only the year. This way, viewers are aware of how current are your photos.

Remember, profiles photos on dating sites are an essential part of your profile. If you want to make an impression or a red carpet intro, make sure your photos, especially your main one, has that wow factor that gets viewers attention. Also, consider changing your photos periodically, especially if you have been on the site for several months. Potential partners typically like to see new pictures of those users that capture their interest.

Avoid Posting Photos that Show Your Personal Information

Never post photos showing private information about you that could subject you to becoming a victim of identity thief, fraud, or other criminal behavior by scammers and others attempting to steal information for their personal use.

So, for example, if you post online a picture of you standing next to your car, make sure that your license plate number is not showing. You may even consider not taking the full shot of the vehicle or blur out the license plate number using photo editing software. The same goes for any other objects that may give away private information on you. For example, if you have a photo taken of yourself outside your home, make sure your home address does not appear in the shot. The same goes for the number on your mailbox and your street name. Maintaining your privacy should always be of importance when posting your profile online.

Select a Username that Reflects Who You Are

When selecting a username or screen name for your online dating profile, consider a catchy name that in some way reflects your personality, interests, hobbies, or even your thoughts. Try to be creative. Avoid having one of those common usernames where 10 to 20 other people on the dating site have a similar username or screen name. Again, you want to stand out from the crowd. You want to distinguish yourself from others and be memorable.

However, reframe from using a username that may scare people away from you, such as Herpesgirl or Serialdater707. Instead, go with something like Affectionate4you or Uhavemyheart2. Have fun coming up with something original but try not to spend a lot of time on something that is not an essential part of your online profile.

Communicate Your Personality, Needs, and Wants

Generally, after a user views your photo on a dating site and finds you worth exploring further, they will then read the written portion of your profile to learn more about you. After your photos, this is the second most important section of your profile. It is your opportunity to put into words your personality, what you're seeking in a partner, and your interests, ambitions, and desires. This is the section of your profile to show that you are more than a pretty or handsome face. It is where you enlighten and capture the reader's interest beyond just the photos you posted.

I have seen many people mistakenly given little attention to the written or essay section of their profiles. There is a myth out there, especially among woman, that men seldom read their profiles, they simply look at the photos. Arguably, yes, more men than women may not read, at least, all parts of women profiles, but it's a low percentage. Men that are looking for a good woman for a long-term relationship do carefully read the profiles of women they find interesting, attractive, appealing, and possibly compatible with them. Such men are looking for a pretty face, but not only a pretty face. They are looking for a woman of substance, intelligence, character, and other good attributes that make those women worth approaching.

Therefore, women and men should give more attention and thought when responding to dating sites essay questions. Take time out to think about what you want to say and how to say it. Consider pondering how readers will receive or interpret what you write. If it sounds too negative or condescending and that's not the meaning you want to project, then rewrite it in another way so that it does convey a softer or pleasant message that you want to deliver to potential matches.

Just how much should you write when responding to essay questions? The best response would be enough to get your point across in an articulate or understanding manner. However, most online dating sites do have limitations on just how much you can write in these sections which you give more information about yourself. So make sure you communicate your message with the available space provided.

Don't forget to refer to your uncompromising and compromising needs list or Compatibility Point Factor Chart when addressing your needs and other desires for the written or essay section of your profile. This is the ideal section for communicating those specific needs. Also, don't be shy about sharing your bucket list or future goals. The reader may have a similar bucket list or list of goals which can enhance your potential compatibility.

Again, make sure your personality is reflected in your profile. For example, a sentence by a woman on her profile like the following gives men readers a sense of her character, interest, and values:

"...I'm an affectionate and emotional being that cares about the homeless and the disadvantaged people in the world. I often give to charity and my church that I attend mostly every Sunday."

It's pretty clear from this woman's two sentences that she is concern about the poor or destitute. Also she cares about her church. Readers of the profile would perceive her as someone that is warm, caring, religious, friendly, and expressive. She seems like the type of woman many respectable men would seek out to know better.

Note also such sentences were written conversationally, making it pleasant to read and understand. This type of writing style makes for a pleasing written profile that gets read, and in many cases, gets responses from readers.

Avoid Sharing Private Written Information in Your Profile

Also, as mentioned about maintaining your privacy when posting photos, the same is appropriate when listing written information in your profile. Do not put personal contact information in your profile. For example, phone numbers, email addresses, websites, and other related information that can be used and abused by scammers and strangers should be avoided at all cost. If you make contact with someone you want to get to know better and are comfortable in sharing your email with, send that person your email address. Later, provided you are content in doing so, you can forward them your cell phone number via your email address. According to FBI and other law enforcement agencies, Americans have lost millions of dollars to online dating fraud. Avoid becoming such victims to scammers.

Proof Read Your Written Profile

What automatically kills a written profile is when it's filled with misspelled words, grammatical errors, and other mistakes. It sends embarrassing messages to readers that you're either careless, which also can be a reflection of your overall personality; or you probably failed classes in English or writing 101.

Therefore, make sure you proofread what you write in your profile before hitting the save or submit button. Use resources such as spell and grammar check that may come with your computer software, or online grammar-checking programs. Also, as mentioned earlier, consider first drafting what you want to say offline, and if the dating site allows you to do so, cut and paste what you have written onto your profile page.

I have seen many written profiles on dating sites with an amazingly high number of errors. It was almost as though the profile writer never actually reviewed what they had written. Avoid making such a mistake. Review your writing and double-check it to ensure all typos and other errors are corrected. Also, if you been on the site for a while modify your message periodically.

Key Points to Remember or Act Upon

- Your profile photos must be captivating and appealing to the eyes; and the written portion of your profile should easily reflect your real personality and other traits.
- Whether you take the photo yourself or have someone else take pictures of you, make sure the shots are not blurry, dark, grainy, or out of focus. Proper lighting is one of the primary keys of good quality photos.
- Remember, profiles photos on dating sites are an essential part of your profile. If you want to make an impression or a red carpet intro, make sure your photos, especially your main one, has that wow factor that gets viewers attention.
- Consider pondering how readers will receive or interpret what you write. If it sounds too negative or condescending and that's not the meaning you want to project, then rewrite it in another way so that it does convey a softer or more pleasant message.
- Proofread what you write in your profile before hitting the save or submit button. Use resources such as spell and grammar check that may come with your computer software.
- Consider first drafting what you want to say offline, and if the dating site allows you to do so, cut and paste what you have written onto your profile page.

Chapter 6

How to Have a Productive Experience on Dating Sites

You developed your Compatibility Point Factor Chart, completed your profile, and posted it on the dating site. You are eager to be a part of the online dating site community. Hopefully, your profile captures the interest of someone compatible with you and is seeking a long-term heterosexual relationship.

Posting a profile on a dating site is a form of promoting and advertising yourself. It's also a way of recruiting what you're seeking in a partner. Therefore, your profile both promote who you are while also advertising what you're looking for in a mate.

Now you must make your promotional, advertising, and recruiting campaign successful. Your Compatibility Point Factor Chart and profile are part of your strategy and plan to find what you're looking for in a mate. But there is still some communication work to do.

Be an Active Participant

You will find on dating sites there are both active and passive users. Unless you are super-fine or super-handsome, an inactive person will generally end up on the dating site for a more extended period, unsuccessful in making many connections. The best approach to ensure that you are making connections with potential matches is to be an active participant. This does not mean starting a conversation with just anyone. It does mean being proactive in approaching someone that you find interesting and possibly compatible with you. Something in their profile, besides only their photos, caught your attention and curiosity. Whatever that captured your interest can be used as an opportunity to start a conversation. Or leave a polite message if they are not currently online.

Many women may have a problem with this approach, especially since women traditionally have been bought up to believe that the man should make the first approach. They may feel that it's not ladylike or it makes them seem too aggressive if they approach the man first. Well, that attitude among some women has changed somewhat, especially on dating sites. Some women in the online dating community are just as quick to approach a man as a man is apt to approach a woman.

To be successful in finding a mate, singles on dating sites must remind themselves that they are on the site to make a connection with a potential partner. The intent is to eventually move off the website to get to know the potential mate better offline. Your aim is not to become a "serial dater" or a long-term member of the dating site; leave that role to some of the casual daters.

There are thousands of people on dating sites; you are sure to find someone that interests you. To motivate yourself to be more active, set a goal. For example, you may aim to leave a greeting message to two or more people a month that meet your interest. Or better yet, if they are online at the time, send them a message in real-time. Such an approach will keep you engaged and communicating among those that may be a good match for you.

If you're not sure what to say in your greeting, read their profile and comment on something in it that genuinely captured your interests. For example, you may say, "Hello, I enjoyed reading your profile, it was well written, and I share your interest in tennis." A short and complimentary message to someone that interests you is sure to compile most to respond in a pleasant acknowledging manner, whether they are interested in you or not. If they are, they probably will follow-up with you with more than a thank you, possibly engage in further conversation with you, including your shared interest in tennis.

Earlier, we talked briefly about those that do not respond to you when you send a message. The theory is if after sending two or three messages to someone that interest you and they fail to respond, then they are sending you a signal that they are not interested. In the online dating community, many that are not interested in you prefer such an approach rather than telling you they are not interested. But you will get some that will be more direct with you in sharing their lack of interest.

Just like life in general, expect some rejections. Be aware that others, even some that are compatible with you, may not think you are a good match for them or they simply may not find you physically attractive. Therefore, move on because many others on the dating site may be looking for someone just like you.

But again, the more active you are on dating sites, the better are your chances of running into someone that is the match you're looking for in a long-term relationship.

Also, many dating sites will allow you to arrange your mail settings so that you can either show others that you viewed their profile or you can prevent them from noticing you looked at their profile. Unless you have a legitimate reason for not wanting others to know you saw their profile, I recommend letting users aware that you viewed them.

Most dating site members want to know which users viewed their profile. Clicking on their profile says to them someone took the time to view it. Whether someone leaves a message or not, it's encouraging to people that other users on the site viewed them.

The Initial Chat

It's true, especially among the women on dating site, the more attractive you are, the more greetings or messages you'll likely receive. I know of a few women that told me they received almost 30 or more messages a day. Sometimes there are messages from some of the same annoying people. Of course, many of the women told me most of them they don't respond to except those that were interesting. Sometimes, these women would block out those admirers that refuse to stop sending them messages when they were asked politely to do so. Thankfully, many, if not all, dating sites have a feature that allows its users to block out people they don't want to hear from again.

Despite how many messages you get, it's up to you whether or not to respond to them. If it's a reply from those you sent earlier messages to, if appropriate, respond to them. If it's from those you did not send greetings to, but you still find them interesting and possibly share similar values; then you may want to respond to those as well.

As for those singles who messages that you respond to and you believe would be worth getting to know, review their profile carefully to determine if you share common interests. You may even want to make notes in preparation for a chat session with them on the dating site. Speaking of the chat session, leave a message asking them when would be a good time to chat online. Don't give out your phone number or email address before actually having a conversation on the dating site. Both men and women should wait until they have exchanged written communications online for a while. Then later, if they have determined that they both have mutual interests in each other; they can move the conversation offline.

Some women are comfortable first in exchanging email addresses. After they get more acquainted and interested in a person, they are later open to sharing their cell phone number.

Remember, whether you are a woman or man, you are communicating with strangers online, and they will continue to be strangers until you get to know them better.

When reviewing someone's profile that you plan to chat with try to determine if they are seeking a long-term relationship as you are. If it's not explicitly reflected in the user's profile that should be among the first questions you may want to ask during your initial chat.

Consider also having your Compatibility Point Factor Chart available should you need to refer to it as you chat. Another option, if the site allows it, print a copy of the written conversation with a user that interest you.

Somewhat like an audition or job interview, without directly seeming so, you are trying to determine if that person through your initial chat is someone of interest worth learning more about. You do this by expanding on what they have written or not written in their profile. The initial conversation is ideal for this form of communication.

If after your initial chat you both find each other appealing and wish to have a follow-up conversation on the dating site, proceed to schedule one accordingly. At this early stage of the initial contact, I would discourage you from sharing personal information. Keep the communication on the dating site until you both are sure you want to pursue each other further.

Online dating is a process. It's best not to rush into anything with a stranger until you have established some comfort and trust level with them, and there are genuine interest and compatibility. You learn and develop this through continuous communication.

Key Points to Remember or Act Upon

- To ensure that you are making connections with potential matches, be an active participant on the site. This does not mean approaching just anyone. It does mean sending introductory greetings to those that are possibly a match with you.
- When reviewing someone's profile that you want to send a greeting to, first check their profile to ensure they are seeking a long-term relationship as you are. If it's not reflected explicitly in the user's profile, consider asking them during your initial chat.
- Online dating is a process. It's best not to rush into anything with a stranger until you have established some comfort and trust level with them. Also, make sure compatibility and genuine mutual interest exist among both of you before getting more acquainted offline.

Chapter 7

Are You Addicted to Online Dating Websites?

Although it's not talked about much, many users on many online dating sites such as Plenty of Fish, Match.com, Black People Meet, and many others may find such Internet sites habit-forming or addictive. Some have used the term Online Dating Anxiety Disorder when referring to someone obsessive over online dating. The name I prefer, however, is Online Dating Site Addiction.

An Online Dating Site Addict doesn't necessarily spend loads of time on dating sites seeking dates, but sometimes they are merely reviewing and admiring profiles with little intent of trying to connect with anyone. In some ways, it's like an entertainment event. They can spend months or even years on dating sites not having gone out with anyone. They go online to scan through photos and profiles and periodically send greetings to those of interest. Others will occasionally go out on dates, but won't necessarily try to establish a relationship with anyone, despite someone being an excellent match for them. Many Online Dating Site Addicts may be lonely singles, craving for companionship, while others use dating sites as a form of entertainment or relief from boredom.

Some Online Dating Site Addicts even scan dating sites while at work. Although this may not be as bad as viewing pornography at the workplace; it still could get you in trouble with your employer.

Whenever you are willing to go on dating sites at work and possibly jeopardize your job; that could be a sign that you may have a disorder or addiction. Whether it's during break-time, lunch or even work hours, an Online Dating Site Addict may routinely scan dating sites with their Smartphone or employer's computer to see who's on the site and whether they received any messages.

Employers do have the right to monitor employees Internet usage, including which sites they visited. Many companies do have policies against excessive usage of the Internet during working hours. Employees found in violations of their employer's internet usage policy; could face discipline, including up to termination. If you are addicted to spending lots of time on dating sites, make sure you are aware of your company's Internet usage policy. Don't allow yourself to lose your job over your obsession with spending several periods on dating sites.

A friend of mine named Sam told me he likes scanning through women profiles just for amusement. When I asked him had he talked with some of them, he said once in a while he would give some of the more attractive women a brief greeting message. But Sam admitted that he liked just viewing their profiles, especially the photos.

When I asked Sam how often he visits a dating site, the reply was at least seven times a day, including when he was at work. He also said when he goes online to the dating site times flies quickly.

"I could be scanning through women profiles and when I look at the clock nearly an hour has passed by," Sam said.

I told Sam that it sounds like he has become addicted to dating websites.

I suggested to my friend that he should find someone on the site that he likes and attempt to know her better and develop a healthy relationship with her. I added that this would help occupy his time on her while kicking his addiction of hanging out on dating sites.

Sam, who was in his early 40s, said he was not ready to get into a serious relationship with anyone right now. Sam added he plans to continue to scan through women profiles on his favorite dating sites to see what's out there before selecting a woman to date regularly.

Such an attitude by Sam is not uncommon by many of those that you find on dating sites. Although many are looking for serious long-term relationships; there are numbers of those on dating sites "on the fence" so to speak. They instead spend unlimited time viewing profiles as a form of amusement and entertainment. Seldom do these men and women attempt to arrange a date with anyone.

However, there are many singles on dating sites that are proactive and serious about finding a partner on dating sites. Many are determined to find a match – but carefully. Still, these singles go online to check out who is online or what new members are on the dating sites. It's one of those daily routines for them, similar to checking their email messages regularly. Such types of regular participants on dating sites would not be considered addicted to online dating sites.

Some people on many dating sites have been members for two or more consecutive years. They have had their membership automatically renewed for several years. It's the perfect medium for them since they don't like to hang out at bars, nightclubs, and other places that may be a bit uncomfortable or intimidating.

It's also not uncommon for singles that meet someone online they liked and dated regularly, to still keep their profile on the site, but hidden. For example, while they spend time dating the person they met, they would make their profile unsearchable; at least, during the "trial period" of their new-found relationship. Should their new-found friend not work out, they simply go back to the dating site and make their unsearchable profile searchable. This process allows singles to avoid having to rewrite their profile. However, if singles find someone they genuinely like during dating, many would delete their profile as a result of finding their match. Others still may keep their profiles in an inactive or unsearchable state until they are more confident that they have met their match.

However, some singles forget to remove their profile; leaving it inactive or active despite not having visited the dating site for several months, or even years. This, of course, could be frustrating to members sending such inactive profiles greetings that never return responses. Usually, such types of abandon profiles would need to be removed by dating website monitors.

As for Online Dating Site Addicts, many hang out on dating sites during late hours of the night. From midnight to up to 2 a.m. or later; you can find men and woman on these sites in large numbers. Even my friend Sam admitted to spending many late nights on these dating sites.

When I asked Sam how he finds time to get up the next day to go to work, he said it was not a problem for him.

"I can stay online until two in the morning and get up to go to work at 7:30 a.m.," he boasted.

Breaking Your Online Dating Site Addiction

When you have an addiction or obsession to anything, the first step in getting over it is to acknowledge that you have a problem. Not admitting that you have an addiction to dating sites; will only perpetuate the problem.

Just as excessive gambling, drugs use, and alcohol drinking can lead to abnormal or bad behavior, so can an extended time spent on dating sites. For example, one can ignore or forget important obligations; leave themselves open to online scammers; and even possibly lose their job as mentioned earlier.

Although being addicted to dating sites may not be as extreme as that of drugs, alcohol, or gambling, it could bring stress to one's life. For example, one can go into a temper-tantrum if their computer breaks down and have to go "cold turkey" for a couple of nights without spending time on dating sites.

The best way to cut down on your time online is to find someone that you can develop a relationship with and focus more time with that person offline. Besides, that's the general intent of many people when they join an online dating site. They want to quickly find their soul mate and get off the dating site to develop that new-found relationship. That is if they are not a dating site fanatic like my friend Sam.

If you have the urge to get online to search profiles several times a day, then give yourself a break from the dating sites. Go on a dating website diet that includes taking four or more days a week away from dating sites; instead, use that available time to take part in offline activities. For example, develop new hobbies, join a club, take new classes, participate in sporting events, exercise, and do some traveling. You will find that while getting involved in these offline events and activities, you may also meet someone of interest.

Possibly due to the proliferation of online dating, we sometimes forget the possibility of finding our match at events and activities that are commonly shared with others of the opposite sex. For example, if you like skating, go to a skating rink. You're sure to find single men and women at the skating rink that share your enthusiasm for skating. Such shared interests make for natural conversations leading up to friendships and relationships. Not only can your offline activities give you opportunities to enjoy other interests, but it also opens up the possibilities of meeting your potential match.

Sometimes singles get so dependent on dating sites for meeting their match that they forget the old fashion ways of finding their potential partner.

People today still meet their future spouse at bowling alleys, parties, work, sporting events, church, clubs, schools, and so many other places. Knowing these offline opportunities are out there for you to expand on your search for your ideal partner is worth acting upon and limiting excessive time on dating sites.

If you find yourself becoming preoccupied with scanning dating sites, aimlessly searching profiles, whether for dates or merely admiring them; consider getting involved in offline activities. Go out and meet new people while also getting occupied in other events, interests, and activities. You may find women and men at these events and activities which may be a better match for you than what you been searching for on dating sites.

There is nothing wrong with spending time on dating sites to meet someone for long-term, casual, friendship, or other types of relationships. It's when you allow your time and energy to become obsessed on these dating sites is when addiction sets in. Consider some of the options discussed to help you limit your time on dating sites.

Key Points to Remember or Act Upon

- The first step in getting over your addiction to dating sites is to acknowledge that you have a problem. Not admitting that you have an obsession with online dating sites; will only perpetuate the problem.
- The best way to cut down your time on dating websites is to find someone that you can develop a relationship with and focus more time with that person offline.
- If you have that urge to go online to search profiles several times a day, then give yourself a break from the sites. Go on a dating site diet that includes taking four or more days a week off the sites. Use that available time away from dating sites to take part in offline activities.
- People today still meet their future spouse at bowling alleys, parties, work, sporting events, church, clubs, schools, and so many other places. Knowing these offline opportunities are out there for you to expand on your search for your ideal partner is worth acting upon and limiting excessive time on dating sites.
- There is nothing wrong with spending time on dating sites to meet someone for long-term, casual, friendship, or other types of relationships. It's when you allow your time and energy to become obsessed on these dating sites is when addiction sets in.

Chapter 8

How to Identify and Avoid Scammers on Dating Websites

Many paid membership dating sites have systems in place to help keep scammers out; some are better than others. Therefore, don't be surprised should some con artists still find ways to slip by dating sites gatekeepers occasionally. For many free dating sites, the gatekeepers may be a little relaxed or not as secure at controlling scammers that occupy their websites. Therefore, when on dating sites be watchful of scammers that can include both men and women seeking ways to defraud unexpected victims from their finances, personal information, and overall identity.

According to an FBI report, in 2016, more than $230 million was lost by consumers as a result of so-called "romance scams" than any other kind of Internet fraud. Also, according to a 2014 FBI report, within six months, Americans lost more than $82 million to online dating fraud. Scammers are on many of these dating sites, and you should not only be aware of this but know some of their behaviors. If not, you can potentially become a part of future scam statistics like those mentioned in FBI reports.

So, when on a dating site, how do you know if you're being "worked on" by a scammer?

There are many ways to tell, but before I go into specifics, let me share with you a true story of a buddy of mine that encountered a scammer while on a popular dating site. To protect my buddy's identity and prevent him from embarrassment, I won't use his real name. I'll call him Fred.

Fred's Encounter with a Scammer

In the summer of 2018, Fred, divorced, age 60, and a Chicago carpenter had considered finding a date on the popular site Plenty of Fish. Weekly he would scan the site trying to find the woman of his dreams without little success. However, one day, he saw this gorgeous brunette with a great smile and perfect body. She had also written what seemed to have been an honest and genuine profile that said she was looking for a life-time partner.

The woman's profile captivated Fred's attention. She was just the kind of woman he had been looking for in his online dating search. She was beautiful, well dressed, communicated intelligently, and shared some of his interests and values.

Fred quickly sent the woman a greeting. He didn't expect to receive a response from her, believing that a woman of such beauty and class probably had 30 or more men responding to her profile. However, to his surprise less than 12 hours later, the woman had returned his message.

After freely giving both her first and last name to Fred, calling herself Molly Simpson (not her real name), the 45-year-old, Naperville, Illinois widow, and real-estate consultant; asked Fred to send her his email address and she will respond to him further. She also promised to send Fred additional pictures of herself not appearing on the dating site. She added that she did not want to communicate any longer on the dating site.

Fred graciously gave her his email address and anxiously waited to hear from Molly.

A day later, Molly had sent Fred a message to his email address. She also included her own email address which was one of those Gmail email accounts. After some pleasant greetings, Molly asked Fred to send her a couple of photos of himself, and Fred quickly did so. Before long, Molly was sending messages to Fred almost every two or three times a week and Fred would usually respond to each of them. When he didn't respond in less than two days, Molly would indicate in her email message her disappointment. This, of course, encouraged Fred to respond to her messages more quickly. He was beginning to like Molly and didn't want to upset her, or worse, possibly having her lose interest in him.

Molly email messages to Fred were long and chatty. She quoted Bible verses to him about faith, love, and hope. She already knew from reading Fred's online profile that he was a religious man and wanted to impress him with her knowledge of the Bible.

After a couple of more exchange of emails messages, Molly asked Fred for his cell phone number, and he shared it as Molly, in return, gave Fred her cell phone number. She even gave Fred the website link to where she worked as a real estate consultant. Although she knew Fred would eventually search the link, this was her attempt to gain Fred's trust.

When Fred did search the website address of where Molly worked, it showed Molly first and last name along with her job title as a real-estate consultant. However, he was curious that there was no picture of her on the website along with her name. But he ignored that small detail and continued responding to Molly's weekly emails.

Less than a week later, Molly phoned Fred as she had promised from Great Britain where she claimed she was visiting a relative. Molly had told Fred that she was half British.

During the brief long-distance conversation, Fred noticed a lot of static in the background, which made it challenging to understand Molly. Of course, this was the first time hearing her actual voice, but it seems disguised and somewhat deeper than he expected; almost as though it was a male voice. However, Fred ignored this and assumed it had something to do with the static on the call and the difficulty in hearing Molly.

The two were now in their third week of emailing each other. Fred was getting anxious to meet Molly after endless emails. But Molly had emailed Fred and said that her cousin in Great Britain had become very ill and she would not be able to return to the Chicago area until her cousin was doing better.

Fred noticed in her email messages she was now calling him "Love of My Life," and "My Beloved." Her emails had become longer and more personal. She was even telling Fred that she was in love with him.

Fred was becoming suspicious, given that they have yet met each other and have only been communicating in writing for about a month now. Even though he did not feel the same way about her, he was feeling close to her after the continued emails. Like her long email messages, he found himself responding to her with long email messages.

After nearly three months of back and forth emails, Fred began to demand that they meet each other. However, Molly said she had to go overseas to have a meeting with some business people in Dubai on a major deal which would make her rich for life and afterward she and Fred can buy a home together anywhere they wish.

Fred disappointed again that he would not be able to meet her after months of on-going delays. However, he wished her luck in her overseas business meeting. But Fred suspicion of Molly was now beginning to grow. In two of her emails, she called him by someone else's name and also repeated something as though they had not discussed it before. Fred felt as though Molly was mixing up her conversations with him with that of someone else. But it was not until Molly asked Fred an unexpected favor that he began to do some in-depth investigation.

While in Dubai working on a so call business deal, Molly had asked Fred to give her his full name and address or his P.O. Box to present as her representative partner in the business deal.

"Honey, while I was accepting this proposal, I only had you in mind as the only one I can trust to use his name and address in the business." Molly wrote to Fred.

She also told Fred not to tell anyone else about the business deal she was working on in Dubai and that she wanted him to send the information requested right away.

"Please send it to me in your response to this email unfailingly. You are all I know, trust, and care for in this present world now." Molly wrote with a sense of urgency.

Fortunately, Fred, throughout his communications with Molly, had never given her his last name or home address. Nor had Molly asked for it during their now three months of emailing each other. All of sudden while in a far off place like Dubai, she desperately wanted Fred full name and address for use as a fake partner to close a business deal that would grant Molly a large sum of money.

Fred did not immediately respond to Molly's email message. Instead, he thought carefully over her message and began to do some real hard digging about Molly herself.

While doing some investigation, he later went ahead and responded to Molly's request.

"I cannot accept being a part of this because I do not know these people you are doing business with, nor was I at the meeting, and they seem to be rushing you into something without legal counsel. Also, you and I have never actually physically met and do not know each other well enough to go into such a complicated transaction together." Fred wrote back to Molly.

Meanwhile, Fred continued with his investigation. He discovered that Molly was not calling him from a cell phone as she had told him when they first started talking by phone. Through a free phone online identification service, he found out that Molly was calling him from a landline phone in the New York area.

Putting all his suspicions together, Fred finally realized that he was dealing with a scammer. He was disappointed in himself for not being aware of it much earlier because many of the signs of Molly being a potential scammer were there. However, like many lonely men and women, he got caught up with the praises and attention given to him. Also, he was enchanted by a beautiful woman at least 15 years his junior showing such keen interested in him.

But Molly's email message to get him involved in a strange deal supposedly to be taking place overseas with strangers was the final nail in the coffin for him. He knew after finding out that Molly lied about calling from a cell phone, that she more likely was lying about other things she told him.

Not realizing that Fred was onto her scandalous operation, Molly emailed Fred to follow up on her request for his personal information.

"Thank you, my love, once again for coming into my life," Molly wrote in her email message. "Money will never be something for us to worry about because we will have an equal share of the proceeds from the transaction. My true love, I wish you a wonderful day ahead as I wait for your full name and address in a return email," Molly message ended.

Judging from her email message, it was as though she had never read Fred's earlier email informing her he would not be a part of her business transaction with strangers in Dubai.

After receiving the Molly's email, Fred returned the following email message to Molly.

"Molly, if that's your real name, I have done some research on you and have concluded that you are actually a scammer," Fred stated.

Fred told her about how she had lied about the cell phone she had been calling him on. He also told her about how she had mistakenly called him by someone else's name in at least two or more her email messages. Fred also mentioned to Molly that she had repeatedly made up excuses not to meet with him after nearly three months of emailing each other. Finally, he told her about how her voice seemed to be in disguise over the phone when they spoke, and there was no verification of her real identity found online. He even told her that he had a suspicion that she may also be a male.

"I can only assume that everything else you have told me is all a lie. I must give you credit and high marks for game playing. But now that I have come to realize that you are not who you say you are, there is no need for any further communications between us. I can no longer trust you. Therefore, you can move on and attempt to defraud someone else. This is my final communications with you." Fred wrote.

Molly never responded. Perhaps she had realized that Fred had exposed her scheme and that it was time to move on to someone else, which is how scammers operate when their victims have uncovered them.

Fortunately, for Fred, he did not send the scammer the personal information she requested, nor did he send her any money during their nearly three months of communication by email.

The scammer also didn't bother Fred again. Perhaps she feared that Fred might contact the authorities on her. However, since Fred lost no money, he didn't bother to report the scammer. Besides, all he knew for sure about the scammer was the phone number she had called him from was in the New York area. Still, the proper thing to do would have been to report the incident. The scammer was probably planning to use Fred's personal information in an attempt to hide money.

This true story about Fred and his encounter with a scammer was to show you how convincing a con artist can be to people on dating sites.

How to Identify Dating Site Scammers

Scammers are all over the Internet, and not just dating sites. As mentioned earlier, many people have lost much as a result of being schemed by scammers. To avoid them on dating sites, be aware of specific behaviors that are commonly used by scammers. Here are among some of their practices: Many posts fake profiles on dating sites to attract your interest. Scammers rarely use their own photos. Many uses captured photos stolen from other people without the real owner's knowledge. Also, some scammer's images are stock photos. Lots of time, you can tell a stock photo by how polished and professionally done it looks.

Many scammers are men preying on women and women preying on men. But also many scammers can be men acting in the role of women and preying on other men, just as women can be operating in the role of men and preying on other women.

Scammer profiles vary in terms of content. Some are excellent and convincing writers, while others are not such good writers and have quite a few errors in their written profile.

These con artists don't necessarily always wait for you to make the first move. They may politely send you a pleasant greeting telling you, for example, how impressive your profile was to them, followed by different small-talk conversation to get you engaged in a discussion. They will later attempt to get your email address, including sharing their email also to move the conversation off the dating site. Once you start communicating with them off the dating site and via email, they may ask that you send them additional photos of yourself. Such additional images can be used in one of their future schemes with someone else.

Many scammers try to find out as much as possible about you during conversations with you via email, text, or phone calls. Yes, they do eventually ask for your cell phone number and even once in a while phone you; many disguising their voice.

Scammers also make you believe that they are unavailable when you attempt to arrange to meet them. They tell you they have an out of town business meeting, their mother is in another state and is very ill, or they have to go out of the country for their company. Speaking of company, they also give you false information on what they do for a living (besides scamming) and the organizations where they worked. Not surprising, they also lie about where they live.

Ultimately they will ask you for a favor which involves either you giving them some money or private information. Scammers will explain some kind of transaction, business operation, or emergency they are involved in and seek your help. Of course, this won't happen until after they have gained your trust. They also will attempt to sell you on the fact that they are falling in love with you, despite not ever having met you in person.

Just like the Molly character in Fred's story, scammers are working on more than one victim simultaneously, so at times they may get your name mixed up with another person they are attempting to scam. This mishap, like all the other suspicious behaviors mentioned, should act as a warning sign to you, and you should cut the so-call relationship immediately. You may want to do like Fred did to Molly and send the scammer a last "Dear John" or "Dear Jane" email letting him or her know you are on to them as a scammer and that there will be no more communication with them. If they persist, then contact the appropriate authorities. Better yet, you may want to contact the proper authorities anyway. Also, send a message to the dating website administrator, making them aware of the scammer.

Many scammers do move on after they have been discovered. They don't want any police action. Chances are they have been reported by someone else anyway.

How to Protect Yourself from Being Scammed

There are several ways to protect yourself online when communicating with a prospective partner for the first time on a dating site. I will focus on some of the obvious and not so obvious. First, don't freely give out personal information during the first time talking to someone. This includes last name, email addresses, cell phone number, work phone number, and other information that can open you up to potential fraud.

Continue the conversation on the dating site for a while, at least until you have developed a trust and comfort level with the person that you believe may be someone worth knowing. After two or three different days of communicating on the dating site, and you feel that you want to move the conversation offline, give the person an email address that you don't usually use. It could be a temporary, newly created email. Should you later find the person not as trusting as you thought, you can easily deactivate the temporary email address. Also, you can put a block on the dating site should that person attempt to re-contact you through that venue.

Consider having a conversation with the person that you met online via video conference call before meeting them directly. For example, have a Skype video-call with them. This allows you both to see each other as you talk. Video conference calls are a great way to verify that the person you are communicating with on the dating site is the actual person in their profile photo. Skype calls are free, so there should not be any excuses for accepting such a call arrangement. If the person refuses, and have no legitimate reason for not accepting an invitation to do a Skype call; then he or she may have something to hide. Also, when you do a video conference call, make sure none of your private information in the video appears on the video that the viewer can see.

If after you developed a comfort level with the person, you have communicated with on the dating site, and have exchanged cell phone numbers, get to know each other gradually before you meet in person. During the phone conversations, consider taking notes. You both are still learning who each other are. You also want to be on guard that the person is trustworthy and honest with you. The note-taking not only help in learning about the person but also ensures they have been consistent in their conversation with you.

After your gain comfort and trust in the person over the phone and you feel assured that they are not a scammer; move forward with arranging a date. But make sure the date is at a public place, such as a restaurant, museum, or even an outdoor event where many other people are present. Also, let a relative or friend know where you are and essential information on the person you are meeting.

Many times our gut instinct will tell us what type of person we are dealing with socially. Most Scammers don't want to meet in public because it exposes themselves to who they are. As mentioned earlier, the photo on the dating site usually is not them. If they were to meet you, whether in person or on Skype, their cover would be blown.

Internet Tools to use to Identify Potential Scammers

Google Images (Images.Google.com) is a great search engine tool that allows users to search the web for image content. Not only can you verify if an online dating site photo used by a scammer is real or possibly stolen, but Google Image Search can be a resource to help determine if someone is using your image without your permission.

Other resources for checking images include TinEye (TinEye.com). TinEye uses an advanced image identification technology to search where an image came from and if there are any more similar images like it.

SocialCatfish (SocialCatfish.com) is another option for helping you verify not only Images, but also validate email addresses, phone numbers, and online profiles. The site use image metadata and facial recognition that can scan millions of social profiles, including social networkers like Facebook, Instagram, and Twitter.

Beenverified.com is another tool for verifying information on someone you may be suspicious of that you met on a dating site. It, like many other research websites, is ideal for doing background checks on people.

Some other reverse image search engines include RevIMG, Yandex, and Image Raider.

Some image and informational search tools charge you a fee to use, but there are also many available that are free. Do an Internet search to explore the variety of resources you can use to check up on someone that you have come into contact with on dating sites.

Some Steps to Take if You Find Your Account Had Been Jeopardized

Should you discover that a scammer has successfully stolen money from your banking account, it essential to act quickly. Here are some steps to take:

- If you find that money has been stolen from your account, file a police report quickly and then contact your financial institution to close down the compromised account. Have your bank or other financial institution to transfer the remaining funds to a new bank account with a different account number and debit card.

- Monitor your bank statements monthly for unauthorized charges, especially following an incident in which your account had been jeopardized. Scammers may share personal information they taken from you with other criminals that might try to access your account or open new ones.

- Avoid sending personal financial information by email.

- Make sure your iPhones, Android phones, and laptops are encrypted. Encryption makes it more difficult to retrieve anything without your permission. This comes in handy should one lose their phone or laptop to bad guys because they will have difficulty accessing your valuable information.

- Consider using different passwords for different accounts. This comes in handy when there is a large–scale password breach. You become mostly at risk when you have only one password for several accounts.

Key Points to Remember or Act Upon

- Many scammers are men preying on women and women preying on men. But also many scammers are men acting in the role of women and preying on other men just as women are operating in the role of men and preying on other women.
- Once you start communicating with scammers off the dating site and via email, they may ask that you send them additional photos of yourself. Such images can be later used in schemes to impersonate you in future scamming activities.
- Video conference calls such as Skype are a great way to verify that the person you are communicating with on a dating site is the actual person in their profile photo.
- SocialCatfish (SocialCatfish.com) is one of many services that verify Images. The site can validate email addresses, phone numbers, and online profiles. The site use image metadata and facial recognition that can scan millions of social profiles, including social networks like Facebook, Instagram, and Twitter.
- If you find that money has been stolen from your account, file a police report quickly and then contact your financial institution to close down the compromised account.

Chapter 9

Some Contemporary Dating Apps and Sites with Different Concepts

New online dating sites and their apps are popping up as fast as McDonald's Restaurants did a several years ago. According to a 2017 survey, 19 percent of brides said they met their spouse on an online dating site. More than 1,000 of these popular sites and their apps are started annually according to at least two reports. The growth of this $3 billion profitable industry has continued not only in the U.S. but also in other nations. Many of these new dating sites, like the most well-known ones, use apps. The app devices allow users to swipe through profiles to select a person they would be interested in getting to know and ultimately date. According to a 2018 survey, the online dating market is expected to grow to $12 billion in 2020. What this means is that the online dating industry is here to stay—at least for a good while.

For those that would like to try some of the rather new dating sites that lack household names like Match.com, eHarmony, or Plenty of Fish; there are plenty among them to consider. Many come with new concepts that distinguish them from many others. Many use apps which for years have been highly popular among several dating site members, especially among the younger users in the 18 to 29 age group. In the U.S. the most popular dating apps in 2018 was those by Tinder (8.2M), Plenty of Fish (6.7M), Match.com (5.1M), and Occupied (5.1M).

But this chapter is about those somewhat new upstarts dating sites and their apps that bring new concepts to the crowded but still growing, online dating market. Below is a summary of those that stand out.

New Dating Sites/Apps Worth Considering

Settleforlove.com is a dating site that was started up by David Wheeler and Jacob Thompson. The website, founded in 2014, has nearly 10,000 users. Those users are in all U.S. 50 states and Canada. It is a free online dating and social networking app. The site differs from many other dating sites in that members are required to upload both good and bad photos of themselves. It also requires them to list both positive and negative traits that they have. The concept is that people are not perfect, and everyone has both positive things about themselves as well as flaws. One must give high marks to both Wheeler and Thompson for their dating app despite its somewhat-awkward, but different and successful concept approach. The focus is to allow people to show their real selves and acknowledging that no one is perfect. People looking for long-term relationships will find this site worth joining. It also appeals to casual daters as well.

Hater is among the more newer dating and social apps. Launched in 2017, the concept of this dating site is that it focuses on things that people share in common on what they hate. Users of this site can swipe left or right on potential matches. There is the ability to chat with their connection on the app. To sign-up, users are required to have a Facebook account. After signing up a basic profile is put up for users which they can go in later to customize it. The sites have over 3,000 topics to choose from, including those on politics, sports, food, and many other subjects. Topics also are updated frequently. Such changes can encourage users to update their profiles with their dislike and like on changing subjects. So, if you dislike people talking loud endlessly in movie theaters, Hater will find someone that share such dislike. Also, if you enjoy ice fishing, Hater will surely be able to match you up with someone who also shares such passion. Users also have the option of swiping in four different directions. Those directions are for dislike, like, hate, and love a person, activity, or concept.

Bumble is another dating and social app with a different concept. Launched in December 2014, this dating app requires women to make the first approach or move in the greeting process.

If a user is messaged after matching with a potential partner and doesn't respond within 24 hours, the match opportunity disappears. The concept of putting 24 hours to respond is to encourage singles to quicken that dating process. Bumble allows its users to make connections for long-term, casual, friendly, and professional networking relationships. Bumble has quickly increased to more than 23 million users. Match Group attempted to purchase the app, but up until this date has been unsuccessful. The fact that Match Group is anxious to buy Bumble says something about the young company success and prosperous future outlook.

A new dating app for black singles is **Meld**. Launched in 2014, it encourages single black professionals to socialize or get together in an upscale environment. To verify that its members are working professionals, Meld uses LinkedIn and Facebook as a resource for checking their status for membership. The site uses such methods for verification because it wants to provide its users with valid information for finding professionals with similar backgrounds. Those seeking long-term relationships with other black professionals will find this dating app worth considering. Users can push a button to indicate they like a particular profile and receive invitations to converse with those people that seem to connect with them. When users find they are equally alike and connect, they can use the site's internal private communication module to get to know each other better. The dating app also hosts social events in Washington D.C. and San Francisco for its members. Meld provides its users with both a free and premium membership. Meld's algorithm relies on a system in which users have mutual like for each other. When users log on the app, they view the profiles of potential matches which they can then decide to like or give a pass on profiles.

Created in 2014, Happn focus is to connect you with those that physically crossed paths with each other during the day and share similar interest such as movies and television titles. The site allows users to contact each other only if they share mutual interests in each other. This is a plus in that you are not being approached by someone that you don't share the same interest. The site app uses GPS to connect its users who cross paths within a specific radius. As of 2018, Happn had about 50 million users. The site has features that allow you to block users and filter matches by gender and age. Instead of swiping, you hit a button to indicate you like a profile. Happn profile photos are taken from Facebook along with a small amount of other information such as education, employment, etc. The app, however, does not post your Facebook page. Happn could be just the right networking app for those that are interested in connecting with those they physically come across in their daily lives and would like to know better.

Launched in 2015, **SparkStarter** is a matchmaking app based in Minneapolis. Its concept is to connect singles that meet through someone that they know and trust such as a friend. By having friends to make a connection for another friend, tends to give people confidence in the matchmaking selection. Of course, not all the time, such matches always work out. However, the concept has merit and is different when compared to many other matchmaking and networking apps. SparkStarter algorithm mostly relies on endorsements of friends to suggest matches of friends. Like many other dating apps, users of SparkStarter swipe through compatible singles. If they find someone they spark within a mutual match, they communicate with them. It is the matchmaking of friends that distinguish SparkStarter from other dating apps. One can sign up for free to find matches for themselves or their friends. Tony Kramer is the founder of SparkStarter. Millennials seem to be this dating app primary focus; therefore, if you fall into this generational group, this app may be ideal for you.

Created by David Gross in 2016, the same year Donald Trump won the U.S. presidency, **TrumpSingles** is a dating site that appeals to those with conservative and Republican values. Its motto "Making Dating Great Again," is a take from President Trump's famous "Make America Great Again," slogan. Initially many of its members were from the Washington, D.C., Los Angeles, and New York area. It's interesting to note that these areas are known for substantial liberal voters. However, they have several conservatives and Republicans in these locations given the thriving membership of TrumpSingles. Of course, members since its establishment have included those from many other states, including people in Canada. The site also has a mobile app that user can search for their match. The bottom-line: If you are frustrated by the lack of finding a compatible partner that shares your conservative or Republican values at many liberal oriented dating sites, TrumpSingles may be among those still somewhat new dating sites to consider.

As I alluded to earlier, features and makeup of dating sites can change quickly. It's best to visit the website or read current independent reviews to find out the latest make up of those that you are interested in joining.

Key Points to Remember or Act Upon

- According to a 2018 survey, the online dating market is expected to grow to $12 billion in 2020. This all says that the online dating industry is here to stay—at least for a good while.
- Many new dating or networking apps come with new concepts that distinguish them from many others.
- In the U.S. the most popular dating apps in 2018 was those by Tinder (8.2M), Plenty of Fish (6.7M), Match.com (5.1M), and OkCupid (5.1M).

Chapter 10

First and Second Dates Are Learning Opportunities

I have always found it puzzling that several singles refer to their first in-person date with someone on a dating site as a meeting. News Flash: It's really a date, not a meeting. Whether it's informal where you get together at a park bench in casual clothes or attend a fancy dinner in dress clothes; both are considered dates. Whenever you schedule a time and place to get together with someone that you potentially like to get better acquainted and possibly develop a romantic relationship with, that's a date; not a meeting. Got it? Now that we have the language right, let's talk about the dating experience and how to get the most out of it when you get together with someone in person for the first time.

Dating should be an enjoyable experience, whether it's with someone new or someone you already met. For those meeting or seeing each other for the first time, the primary focus is to get to know each other better. If you're at a restaurant eating, you can observe your potential partner table manners or lousy eating habits. You can learn what type of foods they enjoy, and, of course, how they communicate with you when you're sitting across the table from them. Is your date looking in your eyes as he or she talks with you? Or are they showing signs of shyness and periodically avoiding direct eye contact?

Yes, you can learn a lot about a person from the first date. This is why it's important when you make a good connection with someone online that you share similar interests and values, at some point, you should schedule a date with them. Arrange a first date with them with the intentions of learning what they are like in person.

Many of us know not everyone we meet online is not always the person they portray themselves to be. The first date is your opportunity to learn if there's a connection between the two of you. On the dating site and even on the phone, you both had great conversations and felt the chemistry that seemed to exist between you. But now you need to see each other in the flesh to determine if all those positive thoughts, waves of laughter over the phone, and other impressionable feelings are real.

First dates help you confirm your feelings and thoughts about someone that you are interested in, but may still have some doubts for some reason or another. The first date helps you to either remove or validate those doubts.

Therefore, you need to come to the date with plenty of conversation leading to questions that you need answers to without sounding like an interrogator.

When I dated my ex-wife, I not only learned a lot about her from the many dates we went out on but also whenever I visited her at her home. I watched how she related to her parents, and they interacted with her. She was respectable and loving to them as they were to her. Observing how one gets along with their relatives and friends can tell a lot about a person. But not all the time on first dates you get to meet your date's relatives and friends. On most first dates it's just you and your date at a public place together; the way it should be. You are out together to have a good time, but most importantly, to determine if you are a good match.

How Long Should The First Date Be?

Some say the first date should be short or no longer than an hour. I believe the length of your first date should be determined on how well things are going. If for example, you both are having a great time together, the chemistry is there, and you are learning things about each other—why not enjoy yourselves! Extend the date. Besides, you are making pleasant memories on your first time out with each other. However, if the date has not shown any signs of a connection after about an hour together, you may want to end it politely. Thank them for their time. Either at that moment, or later tell them in an email message that there was no connection, but you wish them good luck in finding someone that is a closer match for them.

From this point, you move on. Also, don't look upon the date as unproductive or a failure. It at least allowed you to learn that the person you were chatting with on the dating site and later talking with over the phone the last few weeks wasn't really the person you thought they were, therefore, not a good fit for you. In short, the date helped you end wasting your time with someone that was not compatible with you. Now you can proceed to search for that special someone that is a better fit.

How to Make the First Date Successful

Let's say that you like the person that you are out with on your first date. You want to make a good impression but still, reflect your real personality. Simply be who you are, but also show off your social skills (assuming you have them). For example, be friendly, respectful, and conversational. Also, simile, and show a little sense of humor. Whether you are a woman or man, if you reflect these or similar positive characteristics; your date has a good chance of going well.

People enjoy laughing. When you can make your date laugh or smile, that's a good sign that things are going well. Your date will also feel more relaxed as a result of making them laugh.

Having good eye contact during your conversation is always a plus. It shows you're listening with interest to what your date has to say.

There are some topics to avoid on first dates because of their sensitivity and somewhat emotional nature. Such off-limit discussions would be politics, religion, sex, or your ex. Leave these "hot-button" topics for another time, when and if, you have future dates with that person and have become better acquainted. Still, share engaging stories about yourself that allow your date to get acquainted with your personality. However, avoid dominating the conversation; you both are out to learn more about each other and that can't be done if only one of you is doing all the talking. Also, respond honestly to questions. Lying is never good when you are looking to develop a relationship with someone of interest.

The first date will also help you complete more accurately your Compatibility Point Factor Chart for evaluating your date. Of course, you would never bring the Chart with you on your date.

The one that should pay for the date should be determined ahead of time. Although not everyone would agree with me, but the one that initiated the request to go out should pay for the date. Another option would be to split the cost of the bill. After the first date, the person that requests a second date should pay for the date or split the bill again. However, being a traditionalist; if there are future dates, the man should primarily pay for the date.

When You Know the First Date Will Lead to a Second Date

Usually, after spending your first date with someone you met online, you will know far before the date end whether or not you plan to go out with them again.

If during that first date, the conversation is excellent with plenty of genuine laughter and smiles from both of you; chances are you enjoy each other's company and will go out again. Through your distinct positive vibes and interaction with each other, there is high potential that some level of chemistry exists between the two of you and there is an urge to explore each other further.

However, not all the time, such positive feelings are so obvious. Still, you are willing to give it a second date because of some uncertainty. For example, your conversation went well, despite some differences on social and political issues that were unavoidably discussed. But you also share similar taste in music, food, and movies. Such mixed signals inspire you to go out again to give it another try.

So, second dates can be a result of a pleasant and enjoyable time where you connected totally and instantaneously. Also, second dates can be necessary because of mixed feelings about the first date; therefore, going out again to resolve if there is enough chemistry to continue to see each other.

I would encourage anyone that has mixed feelings after a first date to give it another try unless the differences between you are among your uncompromised needs. Remember, your Compatibility Point Factor Chart will reflect those factors that are deal-breakers. Therefore, in a case where you have mixed feelings, and they are not due to your uncompromised needs, then a second date would be appropriate.

For those second dates, where you go is optional. The key is that you both have a wonderful time doing something enjoyable and allow you to continue to learn about each other and possibly grow a new relationship.

A more carefully planned second dates is appropriate for those that need to resolve their differences and determine whether they can or want to develop a relationship. For such couples, the date should be somewhere perhaps less formal such as a picnic in the park, a quiet location near the lake, or a trail walk. The key is to allow you and your date ample time to communicate more privately and casually so you can address your differences and determine if you want to continue to pursue each other, despite your dissimilarities. Also, after a date or two, you should be able to determine whether you like each other as individuals. Sometimes that alone can help bridge the gap of whatever small or significant concerns you may have with each other.

If you can't determine after two dates that you want to be in a possible relationship with someone; then maybe that's a sign in itself that you need to move on.

Dating allows us to learn about one another. That should be your primary focus, especially when you are going out on a date with someone for the first time. Where you go out on a date does matter. You should make sure that during the date there is time spent where both of you can talk directly and comfortably with each other. For example, if you attend a concert where most of the time is focused on the entertainment; make sure before or after the show that you both make ample time talking to each other. This can be at a restaurant, coffee shop, or anywhere that allows you to have each other's undivided attention for conversing comfortably.

A date without productive time learning about each other through conversation does not make for a quality date.

As I indicated earlier, several people on dating sites today call first dates meetings. I suspect they don't want to consider it an actual date until they first had a chance to check each other out; somewhat of a sign of approval before going out on what they feel is a real date. But again, this so call meeting is actually a date, as I defined earlier.

I can remember when I met a woman online several years ago. After several weeks of long phone call conversations, we finally agreed to get together in person. Besides, through those long conversations, we felt we knew each other well by then. She called our date a meeting and suggested it be at a beautiful hotel lobby. Well, in my mind, that was a date, and I dressed adequately for it. After arriving at the hotel lobby, we exchange pleasant conversations, and I suggested that we go to a drive-in movie. With a sly gleam in her eyes, she agreed. As for the movie well, let's just say that we paid little attention to the film. We were distracted by our deep conversation while comfortably snuggled together in my car and periodically kissing one another whenever the feeling came over us.

Most first dates do not usually end up like this unless of course you had been talking for several long weeks and became connected as we did.

I don't, however, endorse waiting for long periods before going out on the first date. It's best to make the first date after you have had a few conversations on the phone or even had some video chats. When you become comfortable with each other, and most importantly, feel that there is a connection as a result of your several communications; proceed with going out on a date.

The bottom line here is that the first and second dates are about spending time with each other to get to know each other better. Where you go and what event or activity you take part in during the date should be secondary.

Key Points to Remember or Act Upon

- You can learn a lot about a person from the first date. If you make a good connection with someone online that shares some of your interests and values, consider arranging a first date with them to determine what they are really like in person.
- First dates help you confirm or resolve your thoughts, impressions, and doubts about someone that you have been only conversing with online.
- If you can't determine after two dates that you want to be in a relationship with someone; then maybe that's a sign in itself that you need to move on.
- People enjoy laughing. When you can make your date laugh or smile, that's a good sign that things are going well.
- A date without productive time learning about each other through conversation does not make for a quality date.

Chapter 11

Should You Date or Marry Someone Much Older or Younger Than You?

During my early to late 20s, I dated at least two women that were much older than me. At that time in my life, I was more attracted to more matured women. As I grew into my 30s, I began to date women closer to my age. I never regretted dating older women. The two I had relationships with were intelligent, attractive, and caring women. However, as I got older, I realized that I wanted to develop a relationship with a woman closer to my age. Someone, I could marry and start a family with, and move into a house in the suburbs.

I consider 10 or more year's difference in age as a considerable age difference between couples in a relationship. When such a significant age difference exist among couples, there seems to be a higher tendency of challenges those relationships will encounter that directly relates to generational differences.

Dating someone much older or younger than you is not a rare thing. Historically, many older men seek out younger women as do younger women seek out older men. My own great great grandmother at the age of 14, in 1879, married a man age 34. Although there was a 20 years difference in their age, they had a healthy relationship and five children born during the six-year marriage. The marriage was short-lived because the husband died during the marriage at the age of 40.

One of the apparent disadvantages among couples with significant age differences is the high tendency of the older partner dying much sooner than the younger partner during the relationship. This, therefore, results in their life together being shortened. Also, if the older partner should not die early in the relationship, they may still be hit with lingering health issues. Such plight could put emotional and financial stress on the relationship.

Early death and health concerns of the older partners in such relationships are not the only issues couples must be aware of when a significant difference in ages exists. There are also differences in generation issues, taste in music, and lifestyles to take into consideration.

There are studies that show many people frown at age gap relationships, especially those which the woman is older than the man. There have been many stories where there have been, for example, women teachers dating or having sex with one or more of their students or ex-students several years their junior. Some teachers are reported to have married their students.

There are also stories of famous men marrying women decades younger than them that have been tabooed by the public. There was Elvis Presley who at age 24 began dating Priscilla Beaulieu who was age 14. She became Priscilla Presley when they married on May 1, 1967. That marriage ended in divorce on October 9, 1973. There was also 22-year-old Jerry Lee Lewis who married his cousin, 13-year-old Myra Gale Brown on December 12, 1957. They devoiced in December 1970 after 13 years of marriage.

Elvis Presley and Jerry Lee Lewis marriage to teenagers much younger than them were highly controversial, partially because both men were in the public eye and their age difference in the young women they married was considered appalling to many during that time period. For Jerry Lee Lewis, the public uproar over his marriage to his young cousin almost ruined his career.

However, today for the average person marrying someone several years older or younger than them is not so controversial, or at least it does not seem to be provided the age differences are not extreme.

When I was living in Indianapolis and dating a mature woman, I had no intentions of marrying her. She already had four kids, and I did not want a ready-made family. Although we never discussed marriage, I don't believe she had any aspirations of getting married either; she was already recovering from a failed and physically abusive marriage. Therefore, we enjoyed spending time together, and life was good. We surprisingly did not have any generational difference as a result of the eight-year gap in our age. Sexually, we were compatible, and intellectually we were inspiring to each other. In short, we were a good match despite our age difference.

Still, some couples with wide gaps in age don't always do so well. One of them, more likely the younger one, may eventually get a roving eye for others of the opposite sex that are closer to their age. Potentially this puts stress on their relationship with their older partner. Or in contrast, the older partner may feel he or she wants to find someone closer to their age. Like many people, we change as we age and go through various stages of our lives where our needs and even our values sometimes change.

In response to this chapter question: Should you date someone much older or younger than you? If you are adults and are compatible in other ways besides your age, such as similar interests, values, beliefs, and other areas; then yes, give the relationship a try. Besides, compatibility is a much stronger factor than age differences as a predictor of relationship success.

Just like everything in life, nothing is forever. If you find someone that is an excellent fit for you but is several years your junior or senior, it's worth giving the relationship a serious try; if it fails, then move on and find someone that is a better fit for you. At least you won't have any regrets for not giving the relationship a try.

Finding one's match is tricky; just ask some of the many singles searching for partners on dating sites. Disregarding a strong potential match because of their being 10 or more years younger or older may not be the right move to make.

Physical and Mental Age Factors should also be Weighed

As I discussed in Chapter 3, we have more than one type of age. There is our chronological age, physical age, and mental or psychological age. Most people put a greater focus on one's chronological age. However, it is our physical and mental age that is the accurate barometer of our real age. I'll use the current U.S. president, as of the date of this writing, as an example. President Donald Trump, as of this date, can pass for someone younger than his age 72. He's healthy, physically looks younger, and is mentally sharp. He also has the energy of someone 10 years younger. Although the liberal media tend to portray him as someone declining in years, in actuality, Trump is alert, quick on his feet, and has a great memory. You can almost say that Trump is the "poster child" of someone that looks and acts younger than his actual age.

So, one should not only evaluate a person chronological age when they are several years older or younger than them; but also assess their physical and mental age. For example, ask yourself questions such as: Are they in generally good physical shape? Are they mentally healthy? Are they mature? Can they communicate well with you? Questions like these should be asked and evaluated to determine whether you want to be in a relationship with someone much older or younger than you.

Sexual Benefits in Age Gaps

There are also some positive sexual benefits among some couples with significant gaps in age. The advantage for older men with younger women is that more youthful women produce longer-lasting lubrication. In doing so, it gives older men that may be slower to reach an erection, more time to "catch up" and make it easier for them to enter younger women as a result of their high vaginal lubrication levels. Also, because younger women are more "tighter" than older women, older men, as a result, sexual pleasure heightens.

As for the advantages for younger women with older men, they enjoy the comfort and pleasure of a more experience and skillful sexual partner. Many older men also tend to provide younger women more attention in the love-making department in terms of foreplay and conversation.

In relationships among older women with younger men, there are also some sexual benefits in such partnerships. For the older women, they are likely to be turned on or aroused more quickly by younger men bodies that are more likely in better shape than many older men. Also, older women may find it refreshing to be sexually active with young men that may not have erection problems that many older men may have.

For the sexual benefits of younger men with older women, there is the skilled sexual knowledge and experience of mature women, bringing younger men more sexual satisfaction. Also, younger men could learn a thing or two about sexual maturity from older women.

However, there are some sexual disadvantages, as well. Where there is a significant gap in age among couples, for example, it may take one partner too long to reach an orgasm. Or an older male may not be able to get an erection. The older woman may produce vaginal lubrication too slowly, frustrating the younger man. So, sexually, there are both pluses and minuses when it comes to sexual relationships among couples with significant gaps in age.

Nevertheless, the so-called May and December couples that have a vast difference in their ages; don't get together for sex only, more importantly, they become a couple because they enjoy each other's company and love each other.

My cousin James, who has since passed, is a prime example of someone who married and had a successful relationship with a significantly younger woman. In 1985, James married a woman named Sheila 20 years younger than him. Despite some grumbling among relatives and friends about the age differences between the two, James and Sheila ignored them and lived a happy life together. The couple did not have any kids born into their marriage. However, they had a very successful marriage that lasted 21 years up until James death in 2006. Two years later, after James died, I visited his widow to interview her for a family history book I was writing. When I asked Sheila what was it that she missed most about her late husband, she quickly said simply "him."

"James was the best man I ever had in my life," Shelia said emotionally. "He was like a father to me, but he was also my husband. He taught me a lot," she added.

There are many successful relationships of couples like James and Sheila, which despite their age difference go on and live a long and happy life together. This supports the argument that it's okay to date and marry someone much older or younger than you. If a person makes you happy, are compatible with you (despite age difference), and they love you just as much as you love them, the relationship or marriage seems fitting.

Putting too much emphasis on a potential partner's age could result in missing out on someone that is an excellent match for you. Therefore, don't only judge a person by their chronological age. Assess their mental and physical capacity. Also, use the Compatibility Point Factor Chart to help weigh their overall fit with you and your values.

Although many of us look for a mate that is closer to our age range, from time to time, we may find someone who is a near-perfect match for us in other ways besides their chronological age. Also, although many may be happier with someone within their chronological age range, like so many other things in life, there are exceptions.

Key Points to Remember or Act Upon

- One of the apparent disadvantages among couples with significant age differences is the high tendency of the older partner dying much sooner than the younger partner during the relationship. This, therefore, results in their life together being shortened.
- If you are adults and are compatible in other ways besides age, such as similar interests, values, beliefs, and other areas; then yes, give the relationship a serious try. Besides, compatibility is a much stronger factor than age differences as being a predictor of relationship success.
- Putting too much emphasis on a potential partner's age could result in missing out on someone that is an excellent match for you. Therefore, don't only judge a person by their chronological age. Assess their mental and physical capacity. Also, use the Compatibility Point Factor Chart to help weigh their overall fit with you and your values.

Chapter 12

Should You Date or Marry Someone of a Different Race?

In the last few years to the present, there have been a lot of interracial couples showing up in television commercials. These couples range from being millennial to seniors. Some of the ads portray them as couples dating or even married. Entire families are also included in some of these commercials, showing the interracial parents with their biracial kids. Often, when there are black and white couples, usually the black is a male, and the white is a female. It's almost like commercial producers are not only marketing to interracial couples, but also encouraging interracial relationships in a promotional way.

I had friends that dated and married out of their race. Some later divorced, while others remained married to this day. I never had an issue with them dating or marrying someone out of their race. If they were happy and their partners were people that genuinely cared for them; then that was fine by me. Besides, I wanted whatever was in the best interest of my friends. I would feel the same way about a family member had they married out of their race.

The Changing Attitude over Interracial Dating and Marriage

Interracial dating and marriage statistics can vary just like data from political surveys and other types of polling information. One thing I have noticed that is consistent about online dating statistics is that Asian women are highly sought after by men of many races on online dating sites. As for men, white men are vastly sought after by white, Asian, and Latino women. Black women, however, typically prefer black men.

Also, there is reliable data that show that more people than in the past are open to dating someone of a different race. These results also seem to be reflected in online dating sites. People still have some biases about getting involved with certain racial groups romantically, but those biases are not as strong as they once were. There are also specific interracial online dating sites that cater to those that are interested in dating others of different races.

A 2015 survey from the Pew Research Center also supports the changing attitude about interracial marriage and dating. For example, among all those in the U.S. that married in 2015, 10 percent were interracial marriages. The survey also reflected that a growing number of adults (39 percent) believed marrying someone of a different race was good for society.

But still, dating someone outside of your race comes with some levels of stares, resentments, and prejudice when you're out in public places. Not all of the time such negative vibes by the public is obvious, but many times the interracial couple can read or feel such a reaction. However, it's not just strangers that sometimes look upon interracial couples with despise; some of the members of these couples families also give them a difficult time or keep their distance from them. So, yes, times are changing in terms of interracial relationships being more acceptable in the dating and marriage environment, but there still is a large segment of the population that have issues with it.

The 2015 Pew Research Center report indicated that Asian and Hispanic newlyweds were the most likely racial groups to marry someone out of their race. For example, 29 percent of Asian newlyweds had married someone of a different race or ethnicity in 2015. For Hispanics, 27 percent of newlyweds in that same year had married someone out of their race or ethnicity. The percentage numbers were less for blacks and whites at 18 percent and 11 percent respectively of newlyweds marrying someone out of their race or ethnicity in 2015.

As one that looks at trends to predict the future, I can see that interracial dating and marriages will continue to grow. Several factors will contribute to that growth, such as online dating. Dating sites give different racial groups more exposure to each other and allow them to connect and meet each other socially. There is also the continuous growth in the changing attitudes about interracial dating and marriage that both the Generation X and Millennial population are playing a role in changing.

But for the most part, the majority of the overall population and races still will continue to prefer to date and marry someone of their race and ethnicity. The majority of Americans want to have children of their own race. They also want to ensure that their cultural heritage is maintained, and many still don't want the stress, discomfort, and hardship that sometimes interracial dating, and especially marriage, can put on their relationship with relatives and friends that may disapprove of it.

How to Make Interracial Dating and Marriage Work

Many of us have our own biases and prejudices about race, and interracial dating and marriage are no different. However, who one's date and marry is their business. If they are of adult age, they have the freedom and right to date and marry whomever they wish. It's their life and their choice alone. Relatives and friends of such interracial couples that are not happy with such arrangement need to get over it. This is America, and in this country, people make their own decisions to who they date and marry. Those relatives and friends of interracial couples that have problems with this, they need to respect the couple's relationship.

I have spoken with some couples that I personally knew that were in successful interracial relationships, some were not married, but living together; others had been married for over seven or more years. They all admitted that they had experienced some negative feedback from both strangers and people they knew, including some relatives. But none of these couples allowed others to deny them from being together and loving each other. They offered several suggestions on how to make an interracial relationship work, and here are some of them:

- **Allow each other to be who they are** – Just because you are in a relationship with someone of a different race you don't have to change who you are.

- **Respect your partner's culture while also maintaining your own lifestyle** – Learn about your partner's culture while also keeping your own.

- **Make your relationship a priority** – Your interactions with each other should reflect how much you love each other and that your relationship or marriage is most important to you. Even more so than family and friends.

- **Respect each other's relatives** – Although relatives and friends may not be overly okay with the relationship, still show respect toward them. This means to treat them with politeness even though they may show some disapproval toward your interracial relationship.

- **Ignore any stares, mumbling, or other negative vibes from others** – When you and your mate are out publicly such at restaurants, parties or other social events; overlook any signs of bitterness or resentment that the public may reflect. Don't allow impolite behavior to ruin the enjoyment of your outing and time together.

- **Communicate on racial issues of concern** – Share openly any problems you may have or experience that has added stress to your relationship. Work on resolving those issues. Remember, you are best friends, and your relationship is a priority. Keep lines of communications open for discussions of such concerns.

- **Be on the same page about kids** – Just like non-interracial relationships; make sure you agree on whether or not to have kids

- **Accept and acknowledge the challenges** – As long as you are in an interracial relationship be aware that racial challenges may always be a part of the relationship, but don't allow it to destroy your partnership. Learn to live with social prejudices on interracial relationships.

- **Avoid the "Guess Who's Coming to Dinner" announcement** – If you and your date or spouse are invited to an event or dinner party by a boss, friend or an associate; don't feel obligated to let them know before-hand that your partner or spouse is of a different race. They can find that out when you both arrive. Sure, your mate and even you may get surprised stares by both the host and attendees, but that would have probably occurred anyway.

- **Keep each other laughing** - Laughter is an essential part of making couples happy. It also relieves stress in relationships. Find the humor in life situations, including interracial matters. Couples that laugh together, last longer together.

Those I have spoken with had many other suggestions on how to make an interracial relationship successful that could fill additional pages in this book, but I think the few listed here were among the best advice.

Like all relationships, whether interracial or not, they require on-going attention and nurturing. What counts in both dating and marriage is the quality of the person. When going into a relationship with someone, you want to make sure that they are someone of good character. As I mention throughout this book, you must be compatible. This does not mean that you have to be totally compatible, but it helps to at least be like-minded on those matters that are most important to both of you. Such as those values that are uncompromising to you. Again, we are talking about long-term relationships. If you have strong objections to being in a relationship with someone outside your race or ethnicity; then avoid getting involved with such a person. However, if race or ethnicity is not a concern, then go into relationships based on whether that person makes you happy and is compatible with you and share some of your values.

Life is short; make sure you can at least potentially lengthen it with someone that is an excellent fit for you.

Key Points to Remember or Act Upon

- One thing I have noticed that is consistent about online dating data is that Asian women are highly sought after by men of many races on online dating sites. As for men, white men are vastly sought after by white, Asian, and Latino women. Black women, however, typically prefer black men.
- Times are changing in terms of interracial relationships being more acceptable in the dating and marriage environment, but there still is a large segment of the population that have issues with it.
- Although relatives and friends may not be overly okay with the relationship, you should still show respect toward them. This means to treat them with politeness even though they may show some negativity toward your interracial relationship.
- As long as you are in an interracial relationship, recognize that racial challenges may always be a part of the relationship, but don't allow it to destroy your partnership. Learn to live with social prejudices on interracial relationships.
- Laughter is an essential part of making couples happy. It also relieves stress in relationships. Find the humor in life situations, including interracial matters. Couples that laugh together, last longer together.

Chapter 13

Should You Date Only Those That Share Your Political Ideology?

When I one day told my adult millennial son that I only dated women that share similar political values that I have, he gave me a grin that implied, "that's ridiculous." But I was serious. I had learned several years ago after a past relationship that if you're in a long-term relationship; makes sure you and your mate share same or similar political values. If not, it could later lead to friction and ultimately destroy the relationship; especially if you're like me and are strongly committed to your political and social values.

Several years ago, I was in a serious relationship with a woman I thought I knew well. Although initially, the relationship started on the wrong foot, we became close, and there was great chemistry sexually, romantically, and on several other levels. One winter, she called me and said that she had missed her period. When we later learned she was pregnant, and we were having a baby girl, I initially had mixed feelings given that I was in my late 40s and had long resolved that I was not going to be having any more kids. However, after giving it some long and careful though, I decided that I wanted us to have the baby. But it was not my decision alone. The mother also had a significant say in the matter. After a lengthy discussion, we agreed that we would have the baby provided that both of us were in agreement in having and raising the baby. Weeks later, the woman that I had fallen in love with decided that she did not want another child. She already had one daughter and didn't want another child, at least another daughter. When she later, in a jokingly manner, told me had the baby been a boy she would have reconsidered; I was both upset with her and disappointed. However her main concerns seemed to be health related. She had difficulty when her first and only child was born. Still, I told her I was against abortion. Ultimately, she proceeded with the abortion and I eventually terminated our relationship. The lesson I learned from this situation was not to get into a serious relationship with someone that doesn't share your similar closely held political or social values.

Since that failed relationship, I have been more selective with women that I get involved with on a long-term relationship basis. If we don't share similar fundamental values; I don't allow the relationship to become serious.

I believe this is an essential principle for those seeking long-term relationships. It will help avoid situations like I had with my ex-girlfriend. If you are not looking for a serious relationship, it's okay to date those that don't share your values because the relationship is casual or not serious. However, causal relationships can sometimes transition to something serious. Therefore, you either resolve your differences or terminate the relationship due to irreconcilable differences.

Some couples with opposing political and social views seem to get along just well. In many cases, these are couples where one or both don't have strong political and social feelings about issues. Therefore, their views on politics and social matters don't usually create relationship tension.

There are other couples with opposing political affiliations that avoid discussing their conflicting views to get along with each other.

However, for many, when you and your partner's political views are in contrast, so can your values. Also when you're dating someone that has political ideologies that are opposite of your own, you can sometimes find yourself in polarized arguments with them. You may also find yourself resenting or disrespecting that person for their beliefs. Life can be stressful for some when they date or marry someone with political ideologies and social views opposite of your own.

Online Dating Sites That Cater to Singles Political Affiliations

There have been several polls that have shown the majority of the political make-up of most Americans. For example, a 2018 Gallup Poll showed that 35 percent of adults identify themselves as conservative, another 35 percent classify themselves as moderate, and 26 percent categorize themselves as liberal. I never learned what the reminding 4 percent refer to themselves.

There have also been surveys that have supported the theory that political and social stances of singles can be a strong predictor of whether they get together and stay together. Many dating sites are aware of the importance many singles place on politics. A growing number of online dating sites are catering to the needs of singles looking for partners that share their political affiliation or views. Some dating sites such as Match.com may avoid setting up a Republican with a Democrat or a liberal with a conservative.

Many online dating sites are making it easier for political like-minded singles to find each other by establishing sites that only cater to their politics. You can expect more such dating sites to increase as the polarization of Americans continues to grow.

For conservatives, online dating sites are growing in numbers. If you are conservative or even a moderate Republican, here are some dating sites and apps that may be a bridge to finding that compatible partner that share your political views and values:

Patrio, a right-wing focus dating app attempts to bring conservatives together. The profiles provide information where potential matches went to school, mileage distance, and other helpful information that help users in their search for a match. Patrio's app, as of this date, is available free on iTunes and in the Google Play store.

Republicans Meet is a conservative dating site that has been around since 2013. It not only caters to conservatives but also those Republicans that may call themselves moderate Republicans. The website allows people to join free, and posting a profile is quick and easy.

RepublicanPeopleMeet also allows new people to sign-up easy. It also, as of this date, does not charge people to register, browse, receive matches, or even flirt. As the name indicates, RepublicanPeopleMeet is a sister site of BlackPeopleMeet, SeniorPeopleMeet, and SingleParentMeet.

Conservative Dating Site targets itself to singles that are committed to traditional values. In addition to being a site for conservatives that are seeking serious relationships, it also caters to conservatives seeking casual relationships or friendships. As of this date, regular membership is free.

Republican Passions is not only a dating site but also a social media site. In addition to helping right-minded focus people find their match, it also provides interest groups, forums, live chats, webcams, and even photo personals. The site also offers to register and to communicate free.

Although ChristianMingle is not considered a conservative or Republican-only dating site; it does have several Christian conservatives and Republicans members that value their religious and political beliefs. Therefore, this site should be considered an online dating site for searching for a compatible mate with similar values.

Not surprisingly, **eHarmony** is also another option for conservatives and Republicans to consider for finding a match of like political ideology. Like ChristianMingle, it's not explicitly targeted for conservative and Republican singles, but it does have many members that have right-leaning focus values. The dating site that has been around since 2000, as profiled in Chapter 4, is ideal for all singles seeking long-term relationships.

Other conservative and republican dating sites and apps to consider are **Conservatives Only** that has been around since 2001; **Conservative Dates; Republican Singles**; and **TrumpSingles,** briefly profiled in Chapter 12.

There are also many online dating sites and apps that cater specifically to liberals and other groups that lean left on the political spectrum. Here is a sample of some of those that are popular:

DemocraticPeopleMeet focus on singles of liberal-minded similarities. Members can review profiles, plan dates, chat, and flirt. The site focus is to develop relationships and connections with Democrat men and women that share similar values. DemocraticPeopleMeet, like RepublicanPeopleMeet, is also a sister of websites such as BlackPeopleMeet, SeniorPeopleMeet, and SingleParentMeet.

Democratic Passions is another dating site for Democrats and liberals. The site has an extensive database of like-minded political focus members. It also is more than just a dating site; it also promotes itself as a social network that is motivated by special interests. In addition to posting profiles for finding dates, members can chat, and meet in open online forums.

Democratic Dating Service looks to connect Democrats and liberals with partners that share their values. The sites offer free basic membership. Basic membership allows users to view profiles and send flirts. If you consider yourself left-wing minded in your political and social ideologies, then this site may be just for you in finding a partner that share your values.

Democrat Singles makes it quick and easy for singles to register for free. Such category of members can search for profiles and view members' photos. To send and receive messages from members, users must subscribe to the site. The dating site goal is not only to provide a forum to help liberals and Democrats connect for developing relationships, but also build friendships.

Liberal Hearts is a dating site that caters to liberals and Democrats. It describes itself as a site that "unites single progressives." The site also has a political matching system that brings together not only liberals and Democrats; but also activists and followers of social issues on animal rights, the environment, and other related concerns of left-wing groups.

Serious Relationship Seekers Should Date Those That Share Their Values

Dating and relationships are complicated. Therefore, why make it more complicated by dating or marrying someone that political ideologies are far different than your own. Especially when they feel just as strong as you do about your opposite political views. There is bound to be on-going conflict. Such a relationship could be a disaster in the making.

But for those couples that are already in love despite their political differences; there are ways to make their lives with each other tolerable. For example, political strategists and media personality couple, Mary Matalin and James Carville have been able to live together and tolerate each other's different strong held political ideologies for decades. Matalin, a Republican and Carville, a Democrat has kept their marriage intact despite their political differences. The couple, like many other couples, doesn't allow political differences to be a deal-breaker to their marriage.

Although it's apparent that I'm not an advocate of dating or marrying someone opposite of my political ideology, there are some ways to make it work in addition to Matalin and Carville graceful way of not making it a deal-breaker. One way, for example, is to respect each other's opinions on politics; allowing the other to get their point across without interrupting, despite how painful it may be. Listening is not only a skill but also a form of showing respect to the speaker. At the end of the conversation, you both will still be allowed to agree to disagree. You also may have learned something new from each other as a result of your political debate or conversation.

Another way to get along with a partner that has strong political views opposite your own is to put greater focus on those beliefs, interests, and values that you share that are not related to your politics. By accentuating on the positive things that bought you both together, you can disregard your political ideology differences.

Growing up as a teenager in Chicago with a family of six; I remember days before a mayoral election hearing my father tell my mother to vote for Richard J. Daly. From my perspective, the way he said it was almost like a demand than a suggestion. I later told my mother when my father had left the room that she should vote for whomever, she wished. She assured me that was precisely what she would do.

Going into a relationship with someone that has different political beliefs than your own is something that you must decide whether it's best for you. If you know that you can't sustain a relationship with someone who political ideology and social values are opposite of your own; despite the other similarities and interests that you share—maybe you need to move on. There are so many other potential partners out there that share your political beliefs and will surely make your life less stressful, at least, politically. But during the dating process, make sure that your potential partner is who they say they are politically, and not who they think you want them to be.

The Compatibility Point Factor Chart discussed in detail in Chapter 3 is a useful tool that helps identify your potential match based upon several factors, including your values, desires, and politics.

When we date people whether we meet them on dating sites, at social events, or other places; it's essential to get to know them. If you are seeking a long-term relationship with someone, make sure they share at least some of your political and social values. However, if you are only interested in a casual relationship, then maybe that person political and social values are not a factor for you.

However, the bottom line is that if you are looking for someone long-term, that's when a potential partner politics may be well worth weighing if you want to seriously pursue them, especially when their politics are very different than your own.

No one will be everything we desire them to be. We have to appreciate the qualities they already have that make them suitable, likable, and loveable to us. For me, sharing similar politics and social ideologies falls into such categories.

Key Points to Remember or Act Upon

- Many online dating sites are making it easier for political like-minded singles to find each other by establishing sites that only cater to their politics. You can expect more such dating sites to increase as the polarization of Americans grows.
- Dating and relationships are complicated. Why make it more complicated by dating or even marrying someone that political ideologies are far different than your own. Especially if that person feels just as strong as you do about your opposite political views.
- There are ways to get along with a partner that has strong political views opposite your own. For example, put greater focus on those beliefs, interests, and values that you do have in common that are not related to your political differences. By accentuating on the positive things that bought you both together, you can disregard your political ideology differences.
- During the dating process, make sure that your potential partner is who they say they are politically, and not who they think you want them to be.

Chapter 14

Attractions that Appeals to us in Dating and Relationships

Most people, when they think or refer to the word attraction, they apply it to physical appearance. However, there are other forms of attraction that we should not ignore. For example, in addition to physical attraction, there are sexual, intellectual, emotional, financial, social, and other forms of attraction. These are all factors that one may possess that draw others to them in an appealing manner.

In the online dating world, photos, and how well the person looks in those photos will be a determining factor in whether the viewer will have an interest. However, for those seeking someone beyond merely their looks, they would take an interest in the person's written profile. The written profile would be a contributing or determining factor of their interest since it would help identify the person in the photo personality traits, values, and other characteristics.

Most people want their mate to be beautiful or handsome, but for some, physical attraction is secondary. For others, they may prefer a partner that is rich or financially secure. Or they may place a high priority on a partner that's funny and fun to be around. Some may seek a potential partner that's highly intelligent and have leadership skills. Others may prefer someone sensitive and caring. So it all comes down to what you are looking for in a mate. There are usually several variables that attract us to someone, other than just one factor. It may be a combination of their kindness, the warm and inviting way they talk to us, the scent of their perfume or cologne, or even the sound of their voice. Such a mixture of attractions can draw us to someone in a positive manner.

Our physical looks will change as we age, but so will other things about us may change, such as our health, needs, and other factors. So, searching for a long-term mate requires weighing those factors that are important to you. We go into a relationship with someone as they are at the present time. But we must acknowledge that they could change in the future from whom they were when they first captured our interest and our heart.

Physical Attraction

Physical attraction usually gets our attention first because it's what we initially see. However, people can differ in what they find physically attractive. An example is that many women prefer men with hair, while there are a sizable number of women attracted to bald men. Also, while many men prefer shapely women with proportionate curves in the right places; some men prefer full-figured or larger women. Therefore, physical attraction can be in the eyes of the beholder.

Physical attraction alone should never be the sole factor for deciding upon a mate. A man or woman physical attraction will not singly make their partner happy. Other attracting qualities are warranted, especially in serious or long-term relationships. For example, a man may have a gorgeous wife, but if she is a lousy cook or housekeeper and nags him often; her physical beauty somewhat fades in his eyes. In some ways, her flaws in those other areas can reduce the impact of her attractive physical appearance on her husband. So, for those that seeking a long-term partner that is beautiful or handsome, make sure they have other meaningful attracting qualifies that enhance and complement their good looks.

Assessing a person's physical appearance alone is like judging a book by only its cover. To determine the true value of a book, you need not only view its cover, but also look at the table of contents, read parts of the preface, and scan through its pages to get a better understanding of the book content and quality. A similar process is necessary when assessing the character and quality of a potential mate. Although the person in the profile looks dazzling physically, but just who are they inside. To find out you first need to read their profile, and if further interested, send them a message to establish contact with them. Should you later communicate with them, you will want to ask questions that will give you more insight into their personality and character. Just because they have a beautiful smile and warm eyes in their profile photo, does not mean they are the right person for you. You need more information about them that their written profile may not provide. Physical attraction is fine, but more internal revealing qualities must also be identified to determine if the person is worth considering as a strong potential match for you.

Sexual Attraction

Like physical attraction, sexual attraction is primarily associated with the outer appearance of a person. Many times, when one is physically attractive to another, they may become also sexually attracted to them. Again, we are talking primarily of the opposite sex. However, if one is gay, they can also become sexually attracted to one of the same sex.

A man can become sexually aroused or attracted by the way a woman walks; the shape of her behind or other body parts; or even how she smiles. For a woman, she can become sexually attracted to a man for the same reasons. But physical qualities are not the only stimulus for one to become sexually attracted to another. Other features can bring on an impulse of one wanting to be intimate with another sexually. For example, a person can become "turned-on" by the intellectual appeal of another. Such as an adult student being so impressed with their teacher or tutor knowledge, they become attracted to that person sexually.

Like physical attraction, what a person finds sexually attractive, especially in long-term relationships, will not alone make their relationship happy long-term. A woman may find a man sexually attractive while at a nightclub. But after spending a one-night stand with him in bed, she may later find that same fellow sexually boring and personality-wise objectionable. It was the unknown and image in her mind that initially made the man seem sexually attracted to the woman. But that attraction quickly died in the bedroom during their brief sexual encounter.

When I give the above example, I think of the rare fling I had with a woman I met at a nightclub in Chicago. If I had seen the same woman on a dating site, she would not have been someone I would have had an interest. Sandra (not her real name) was a smoker, cheating wife, freely used profanity, and at times argumentative. However, we were both in our early twenties, and what we did have in common was a sexual attraction. From the moment we started talking at the bar, we knew we were going to be spending lots of time together; regardless of how incompatible we were otherwise. We both knew that our relationship would be purely sexual. We had no intentions of having a long-term relationship because we knew that it would not last long anyway. Eventually, Sandra moved to a small town in Arkansas, where she inherited a house from a deceased relative. It was at that point we ended our fling and had no further contact with each other.

There are many people on dating sites that tend to exhibit their sexual charm by showing photos of them in inviting ways. Some even present themselves in their pictures in positions to imply a desire to have sex or to arouse the viewers sexually. For those that are looking for casual relationships, such persons may be tempting and interesting to them. But those looking for a serious relationship, this would generally not be the type of persons they would be interested in dating.

In a long-term relationship, sexual attraction is a great quality for you and your partner to have. But again, like physical attraction, it's not the only factor to have to sustain a serious relationship.

Intellectual Attraction

Those that are smart, expressive and display lots of confidence can draw people to them based on Intellectual appeal. If you are among those that lack intellectual appeal, you could find yourself attracted to those with such a quality. But others that are also smart and scholarly may find those with similar qualities appealing. As that old saying goes—like minds are attracted to each other. Again, we are referring to attractions among heterosexuals.

Men and women that are attracted to one another's intelligence may find themselves wanting to spend more time talking with each other. For example, a person may find it very stimulating to spend time around a smart person of the opposite sex who is very knowledgeable about historical events. Or there may be, as mentioned earlier, a teacher or tutor relationship which the student becomes attractive to the teacher or tutor for their knowledge.

Many of us want a partner that is smart, articulate, and display confidence in themselves. Whether we lack such qualities in ourselves, we find them intriguing as a potential partner and tend to want to know them better as a result of their intelligence.

In seeking out a mate with desirable intelligence, one must be honest with themselves and ask is such a person compatible with them. Sure, you are attracted by their knowledge but are they a good fit for you. In other words, if you lack sophistication and are not as smart, would a serious relationship with someone with such fascinating qualities be sustainable. It is possible, provided other attracting qualities make you both a stronger match. It all comes down to looking at more than one type of attracting quality when assessing a potential partner.

Emotional Attraction

If you connect with someone that you are emotionally attracted to that can be a positive thing providing the bonding is real and sincere. When you are emotionally attracted to someone, you find that person easy to talk with and trust. You are more open to that person and have a desire to be in their company because of the positive vibes you get from them. Their presence, how they listen to you and interact with you in general allows you to talk about things perhaps you would not talk about to others. This is among those attractions that give a real sense of compatibility. It consists of reliable attributes that are essential to sustaining a serious relationship. If you connect with someone, whether online or offline in the dating world that brings out your emotional attraction to them, that person should be someone worth exploring further. Potentially, that person could be a strong match for you, but they must also in return feel some positive connection with you if the attraction is to be mutual.

Finding someone with such connecting qualities would require communicating with them to an extent to pick-up on whether emotional attraction exists. Also, that attraction would be acknowledged by how comfortable and trusting you feel with that person as you converse with them. The key also is to know and understand what real emotional attraction is and make it a constant judging factor in your efforts to identify a potential partner.

I would be remised if I didn't mention that emotional attractions do not necessarily lead to romantic relationships. For example, you can have a great connection with someone you met and that emotion attraction exist, but it lacks other attractions, such as physical attraction. The person may be comfortable to talk with, such as a good friend, but romantically, there is no connection. Although that does not mean it can't be, for that to happen, other attracting factors may need to exist or become present later in the relationship. If not, the relationship may end up being platonic.

Still, finding someone that you connect with emotionally is a crucial factor in identifying your potential match along with other attracting factors. In the interesting environment of dating and relationships, it takes a combination of factors to predict that a healthy relationship will exist among two people.

Financial Attraction

Not surprising, some date and even marry others for their wealth. There are both men and women that seek out partners for the financial support they can provide them. They may not, in particular, have a strong interest in them personally. But they are attracted to the wealth that an individual could potentially bring to them if they were in a relationship. In essence, they are more interested in a person's money than the individual. If the person being pursued were not financially secured, his or her pursuer probably would not have shown interest in them.

There are dating websites which cater to women and men seeking wealthy partners. Among them are names like Cougar Life, Date a Rich Woman, Date a Billionaire, Luxy, Sugar Daddie, Millionaire Match, and so many others. Some of these sites require both partners to have a certain sum of financial wealth, while others do not.

There is no sin against seeking a partner for financial reasons, although I question the morality of it. However, if you want the relationship to have more meaning than just its financial purpose; make sure the relationship involves other types of attracting factors.

Also, if you happen to be the rich one, avoid showing off your wealth if you have no desire to get involved with someone that wants to be with you primarily for your money. For example, don't post photos of yourself on dating sites sitting in an expensive car or wearing lots of pricy jewelry. You could find yourself a target of those that prey on affluent people.

Many of those that are single and financially stable seek out others that are also financially secure. They are coming into a relationship which both individuals are wealthy. Therefore, there is less of a tendency of their financial prosperity being the primary focus for getting together.

Money issues are among the leading reasons why relationships, including marriages, fall apart. Often the money issue has to do with a lack of it. Having wealth helps to avoid many money problems, but not all of the time it's the answer to a successful relationship. Other attracting qualities should also exist. If you are seeking long-term relationships, make sure your financial attraction to a mate is not a distraction to other forms of attractions they may have.

Social Attraction

There are so many other attractions that we look for in a potential partner. Social attraction is another magnetism that many likable people possess. People are attracted to them because of their popularity, ability to capture others attention, and their great conversational skills. Those that possess social attraction will usually be popular at social gatherings such as parties, reunions, business meetings, and other social events where there are a gathering of people.

Many people enjoy being in the company of those that have social appeal. They enjoy being around such people because of their magnetism and charisma. Those that have social attraction also open up doors for others to meet new people as well as new opportunities.

People with social attraction are easily able to initiate with others. They are very comfortable in talking face-to-face with others and making them feel relax, whether at business meetings, parties, or other social events.

There may be some drawbacks to dating or being in a relationship with someone that is socially attractive. For example, their popularity may sometimes become annoying or envious to you because of the large amount of attention they get; sometimes making you feel left out. Or you may become suspicious of others that may take up much of your socially attractive partner's time and attention; therefore, leaving both of you with little time with each other.

Key Points to Remember or Act Upon

- Physical attraction alone should never be the sole factor for deciding upon a mate. A man or woman physical attraction will not singly make their partner happy. Other attracting qualities are warranted, especially in serious or long-term relationships.
- In seeking out a mate with desirable intelligence, one must be honest with themselves and ask is such a person compatible with them. Sure, you are attracted by their knowledge but are they a good fit for you.
- Emotional attraction can be a good thing for those seeking long-term relationships. Whenever you are emotionally attracted to someone, you find that person easy to talk to and trust. You find yourself being more open to that person and enjoy being in their company because of the positive reaction it has on you emotionally. This is among those attractions that give a real sense of compatibility.
- Avoid showing off your wealth if you are among those that have no desire to get involved with someone that wants to be with you primarily for your money. For example, don't post photos of you on your dating profile sitting in an expensive car or wearing lots of pricy jewelry.

Chapter 15

20 Qualities Key to Your Relationship Being Healthy

Throughout this book, I have discussed ways to make your relationships successful. This chapter expands on that by identifying essential qualities all relationships must have if they are to be prosperous. Here are 20 vital traits that couples must-have for a healthy relationship. They are listed below in alphabetical order followed by a discussion on each. I encourage you to practice and incorporate those that may be missing in your relationship. All of these suggestions and traits will play a positive impact on your relationship with your partner. The 20 essential qualities are:

1. Acceptance
2. Affection
3. Attraction
4. Best Friends
5. Commitment
6. Communication
7. Compatibility
8. Compromise
9. Faithfulness
10. Honesty
11. Humor
12. Kindness
13. Likability
14. Love
15. Reliability
16. Respect

17. Romance
18. Sex
19. Time
20. Trust

Acceptance

Having compassion and acceptance of our partner's short-comings can reflect how much we love them despite their small but yet annoying behaviors or habits. Remember, neither you nor your partner is perfect. Also, be grateful that the little bothersome traits that your partner has are not as extreme as being under the influence of alcoholic or drug addiction. Such types of behavior problems are more troubling and harmful to your relationship than, for example, your partner's rude belching habits. Learning to live with our partner short-comings is about loving them for who they are and understanding that they are human and have faults like all human beings.

Don't misunderstand me; it's okay to ask your partner to put the cap back on the toothpaste tube after using it. However, if your mate continues to do this despite your repeated reminders, it's time to accept your partner short-coming on this matter, and recap the toothpaste yourself. Or buy toothpaste that allows the cap to flip open and dispense the toothpaste without actually removing or separating the lid.

But quirks and annoying habits of your partner are not the only things you must acknowledge about them. You also need to learn how to accept their physical shortcomings. For example, if your partner gains weight and despite efforts to lose it falls short; you both must accept that he or she may have an ongoing weight problem. Not everyone can lose weight like others. Sometimes due to medical reasons or simply one's inability to maintain a certain weight are causes. You don't want your partner to feel that you no longer love them because of their weight problem or whatever other physical problems they may have.

For some, accepting their partner's physical problems such as being overweight can be a challenge to the relationship. However, if you love them, something such as being overweight, lost of an arm or a leg, should not threaten your relationship with that person. They are still the same person you felled in love with, just physically they have changed.

Learn to accept your partner's physical shortcomings, and other flaws, weaknesses, and quirks. Acknowledge and appreciate that your partner positive traits outweigh the negatives ones and is among the many reasons why you are both together as a couple.

Affection

Throughout a couple's relationship, both must regularly show affection toward each other. When you demonstrate affection to your partner, it says to them that you care and adore them. It also shows that you enjoy being in their presence and making them feel appreciated.

Generally speaking, women may show a higher need for affection than men. For many women, if the men in their life do not regularly show loving signs of appreciation and expressions of love and tenderness; they may start to feel less appreciated and possibly alienated by their partner. This feeling of isolation is especially true when women are accustoming to frequently receiving loving and caring interaction from their partner.

For many men, affection is also important, but they generally may not place as high of a value on it as the women in their life. During the early stages of dating, many couples are a little more reserved in showing their affection. Such lack of show of affection may be understandable, especially if you have been on only one date with each other. However, as the relationship grows, that is the time when showing one's affection toward the other becomes more likely. Such display of affection as holding hands while walking; rubbing the other's arms, or calling one up to tell them how much they have been thinking about them throughout the day are all delightful ways showing your partner that you care about them.

For both men and women, when they are affectionate to their partner, they automatically add deposits to their partner's Emotional Love Bank (a metaphor illustrating how we affect each other emotionally through our interactions). And the more affection they give their partner, the more they increase deposits to their mate's Emotional Love Bank.

For some women, when they receive less affection from their mate, their appetite for sex can decrease. That saying that applies to woman: "Without affection, there is sexual rejection," has some truth to it.

Affection between couples can also set the mood for future sex. Besides, it can be difficult for either partner to reject the other's desire for sex after regular days and weeks of displaying affection in a variety of ways. Gifts of flowers, "I love you" calls from work, and other exhibits of affectionate help to energize couples need to become more intimate.

Swarm your lover with affection will make your relationship exciting, healthy, and romantic. The wonderful thing about showing affection is that it does not have to be something that cost you money. A simple kiss, backrub, or even kind words in an email message, are all ways to show your partner you care about them.

If you want affection, it pays to be an affectionate person. In other words, affection works two ways. One must be willing to show affection to their partner if they are expected to receive tender loving care in return.

Attraction

Here, we're talking about physical attraction. Most people, to connect with a potential mate, there usually must be some level of physical attraction if there are to be a chance for them to develop a personal or romantic relationship with each other.

Yes, physical attraction means a lot to men, but so does it has importance for women. Usually, beautiful women and handsome men on dating sites get more messages compared to not so attractive women and men on dating websites.

It's a person's physical presence that captures one interest on dating sites and prompts them almost instantly wanting to view their profile further.

Ask women what they look for in a man, and the word good looks will come up along with terms such as honesty, tall, financially secure, and other related traits. Men will almost always list a woman beauty among their desired wishes for a mate. It does not mean men and women are shallow; it does mean that physical attraction generally is essential to both sexes in selecting a mate.

For a man, his woman's beauty is his pride and joy. In other words, her beauty brings him satisfaction and happiness. When a man has a physically beautiful woman in his life, it makes him feel good about himself. He takes pleasure in her being with him in public, and it gives him confidence in himself that he was able to capture the heart and interest of such a beautiful woman.

Women also share a similar feeling when they have a handsome man in their life. They feel good about themselves that they can have and hold a good looking man that other women would desire. Whether they admit it or not, women also like to show off their handsome man in public.

However, for both men and women with good looking partners, they must also be somewhat attractive. Many attractive people prefer that their partner also to be beautiful. Of course, there are exceptions given that we all have seen average or unattractive women with handsome men and ordinary or unattractive men with beautiful women.

Physical attraction does not necessarily mean you have to be born with it. Little things such as changing one's hairstyle or losing weight can improve some looks. Or for more significant changes, there is plastic surgery as an option.

The media also puts much emphasis on beauty in our culture. Besides, when was the last time you saw an unattractive woman in an automobile commercial selling cars? Also, notice how dating websites promotion photos only usually show attractive men and women in their advertising pictures.

Many single men and women will typically seek someone that appeals to them physically, but it's not the only factor. What all those in the dating market should do is to make an effort to look their best. Not only when dating, but also when in a relationship or married. Again, physical looks mean a lot to your partner.

Best Friends

If you can't honestly say that your mate is your best friend, then you may want to reevaluate your relationship with them or even consider finding a new partner.

At the core of your relationship with your mate should be a strong-rooted friendship. Why is this essential to your relationship? Well, it will be one of the keys to holding your relationship together. There are many cases where friendship among couples can outlast their romantic relationship. But just what is a best friend? It has many meanings for us, for example, a best friend is:

- Someone that you can consistently depend upon
- Someone that you can trust
- Someone that you can discuss any problem with
- Someone that enjoys laughing and talking with you
- Someone that makes you relax and smile a lot
- Someone very honest with you
- Someone that offers comforts and emotional support
- Someone that provides help when it's needed
- Someone that you enjoy being around
- Someone that attempts to put you in a good mood
- Someone that always has your best interest at heart

Based on the above incomplete list, a best friend has many positive meanings for us. Ideally, such traits that make up for a best friend are those that we should look for in a partner.

Best friend relationships are lasting. They make sacrifices for each other and don't complain about it. Best friends have a special bond that is difficult to break. Initially, a friendship develops over some time. Later, it becomes not just friends, but best friends. When you can say that your mate is your best friend; your relationship is practically guaranteed to be healthy and lasting.

When you and your partner are in a relationship, you're learning about each other and as a couple, growing together. Also, as a couple and best friends, you accept and know the other's real self; there is no need or purpose to act a part, nor is there a need for insecurity.

During the early stages of the dating process, couples may want to focus first on establishing a friendship with the person they are dating before immediately creating a romance with each other. However, I would still recommend showing affection and fondness of that person to avoid becoming just a platonic relationship.

If men and women during the initial dating process can determine at a certain period through conversation and time spent together that they have good chemistry and connect romantically; it is highly unlikely that their establish friendship will evolve into a platonic relationship.

Strive to be your mate's best friend, and you are sure to notice the strength in the relationship.

Growing up in a two-parent household, I saw how my father and mother were not only married, but they were best friends. They talk lovingly with each other; even gave each other playful names. They also laughed and clowned around with one another. Yes, they did argue periodically as many couples do, but usually, such disputes would quickly end, and the next thing they were talking and laughing again. My parents were a classic example of couples being best friends.

If you and your partner can not honestly say you are best friends, make a strong effort to nurture your relationship so that you grow into becoming best friends. I can guarantee that you won't regret it!

Commitment

For a couple's relationship to grow and strengthen, both in that relationship must be willing to work extra hard in making it work. When one partner is not ready to commit totally to their relationship, it makes the committed partner feel rejected. They may also think that it would be a waste of their time if they are committed to the relationship but not their partner.

However, abandoning the relationship prematurely may not be the best approach. Sometimes when one partner is putting in a significant amount of effort in making a relationship work, more so than the other; the less committed partner could later turnaround and begins putting in more effort. He or she has seen how important and committed that their partner is to make the relationship work; could later be encouraged to give more serious effort to their relationship.

Although this approach by the person that is fully committed to the relationship may not be natural for everyone in such a situation; it is worth the effort.

Show your less committed partner that you don't consider the possibility of the relationship failing. Do all the little things that show your relationship is a priority and you are willing to go far above expectations to make things work. If after an adequate period, your partner still does not turn around and show they also are committed to the relationship, you can at least take comfort that you had given it your best shot.

Being in a relationship where both partners are committed to making it work brings both comfort and security to the relationship. It strengthens the couple's trust and confidence. There is less of a tendency of jealousy situations popping up or thoughts of infidelity. You have two people working as a team in making their life with each other wonderful, loving, and happy. Commitment to each other has a way of bringing out positive energy and high expectations in a relationship.

How does commitment apply to those starting a new relationship? For example, let say you met someone on a dating site and you went out a couple of times. You found that you are compatible and have great chemistry. The next step would be the courting process. This includes not only spending more face time with each other, but also calling, emailing, or texting each other daily to communicate. Also, you may want to surprise each other with small gifts that bring a smile on each other's face. All of these actions are a display of both showing they are committed to the relationship. Spending adequate time with your partner, talking with them, bring smiles on their face or making them laugh; are ways to tell that person that they are important to you and you are committed to them as your partner.

When you are in the dating market seeking a serious relationship, focus your dating efforts to those that are more interested in a long-term relationship as you are. This way, you have a better chance of finding someone interested in a committed relationship same as you.

Communication

Not surprisingly, communication is high on the list as a quality that is essential for successful relationships—not just any kind of communication, but good daily conversation. Whether your relationship with your mate is new or not, couples should have regular discussions about anything and everything.

Couples need to spend periods talking with each other to stay bonded and in tune with one another. This includes both speaking and listening to each other and giving their undivided attention. But conversations should also be playful and enjoyable.

When I interviewed a couple, a few days before their wedding, the groom-to-be, Rick, mentioned that he and his fiancée, Margo, took time out each evening after work just talking to each other.

Regardless of how tired one or both were, they religiously sat down to connect verbally and emotionally.

"Marcus, no matter how rough my day was or how bad of a mood I was in, Margo would say something funny to me during our evening talks that would bring me out of any bad mood I previously was in at that time. We enjoy talking with each other," Rick said.

When I later interviewed Margo, she repeated what Rick had told me about their daily conversations.

"We don't answer the phone, and the television is turn off when it comes time for our evening conversations," Margo said. "As a result of our daily conversation, we have grown so close and in love," Margo said with a bright smiled on her face.

I also smiled in admiration. I was impressed not only by their devotion and love for each other but how they were committed through their communications to making the other happy and showing how much they care for each other through conversation.

Both Rick and Margo knew how much communication was essential to their relationship. It kept them grounded. The conversations helped them grow together as a couple, and further enhanced their love for each other.

Without frequent communications among couples, relationships tend to lack intimacy, closeness, and connection. When there is a little conversation among couples whether they are living in the same household or not, there are opportunities for them becoming distance both mentally and physically.

Through frequent conversations with someone you are personally and romantically involved with, you promote closeness and intimacy. It allows you to understand and know each other better. When you talk with your partner every day, you both bond together as a couple. The conversations enhance the closeness of your relationship.

As mentioned before, communication for women with their partner is highly important. It not only unites them with their mate but also enhances their enjoyment of sex with their partner.

How men and women communicate differently has been written about a great deal. However, despite some of those differences, there is no excuse for not being able to talk regularly with the person that you are romantically involved. A conversation with your partner requires respect, listening intently, and verbalizing your thoughts without dominating the conversation. When you listen to your partner without interrupting, you show them how much you value what they have to say. Also, if your partner says something during the conversation that was not clear or understood by you, ask questions for clarification.

I had periodic tendencies of interrupting someone when they were talking to me; not only in personal relationships but also business relationships. I was so anxious to get my point across that it affected my listening skills. Fortunately, I was able to overcome this bad habit by avoiding interrupting others when speaking and listening more carefully. I also learned to better converse with my mate.

Whether your partner is less or more talkative, allow them to share their thoughts and feelings without interrupting freely. When you do this, you not only become a better listener and conversationalist, but your partner is more willing to confiding in you. This level of communications is essential for a healthy relationship.

Compatibility

When men and women view profiles on dating sites, they subconsciously evaluate the person compatibility with them. They also do the same when offline at social events such as at parties, sporting events, and other social gathers. They exchange greetings and smiles, but during the preliminary meetings, it is too early to know whether that person that captured their interest is a good fit for them. Although sometimes it can be quite apparent that one is not compatible with them.

When you are compatible with someone that interests you romantically, it provides a jump-start advantage to the relationship. For example, you may have similar social and political values. Or you may have similar interest in recreation and culture activities. Such common interests and likeness are valuable and an obvious sign that the relationship is worth pursuing.

I learned a long time ago that it's an advantage to be in a relationship with someone that shares your interests, tastes, and values. Not only are you happier in such a relationship, but the percentage of your partnership lasting is higher as opposed to one who has significant different interests and values. When you and your partner are compatible, you are in better harmony with each other.

To determine the level of compatibility a potential partner is to you, it's essential that you know who you are in terms of values, beliefs, interests, and goals.

To be compatible does not mean you cannot have differences in a relationship. For example, a couple may share the same religious beliefs, money management values, and child upbringing philosophies; but may differ on politics, housekeeping habits, and other matters. If for example, a couple that shares similar strong religious values but not the same political ideologies; it would be their religious values that are most important to them and would still make them compatible from a religious standpoint.

The Compatibility Point Factor Chart, discussed in Chapter 3, functions as a tool to help you weigh the factors or traits that are most important to you in a relationship. It also helps you to evaluate potential matching partners on dating sites that have or lack factors that are important to you.

While our looks, age, and health may change over time, our strong beliefs and values generally stick with us. This again is why compatibility should be among the significant factors you should consider when determining if someone you are interested in building a life with is the proper fit for you in a long-term relationship.

When I think of compatibility among couples, I again think of my parents. Despite how much they loved each other, they also argued. They were not heated arguments, but more like a verbal disagreement over things like getting the plumbing fixed or putting a bet on a lousy horse at the race track. Such arguing or complaining was part of their communication style with each other. To an outsider, this may seem like too much drama; but for my parents, this was how they communicated. They were not only compatible in terms of their communication style, but also so many other ways. Had they not shared strong compatibility in their relationship, their relationship would probably not have survived. However, my parents remained married to each other for the remainder of their lifetime.

There are times in some relationships when one or both partners behavior may dramatically change. In such cases, the laughter, kidding around, and conversation dries up. To save a relationship may require some outside help such as counseling. Also, the couple must work in cooperative efforts to bring back the energy, happiness, and communication that gave their relationship potency. If compatibility cannot be restored, a couple may have to go their separate ways when all attempts to salvage the relationship has been exhausted.

Make sure whomever you share your life with romantically, that compatibility exists and remains. It is the "glue" that bonds and strengthens relationships.

Compromise

Whether married or not, when couples are in relationships with each other, they will find themselves making compromises on various things that they may have a difference of opinion. Whether it's where they want to go on vacation to what type of house they want to buy; many decisions they make will involve compromises.

For some, compromising is not always easy; especially for those that have been single for a long time and accustom to making decisions on their own. Also, those with Type-A personalities may struggle with compromising. Still, those in relationships must learn how to compromise with their partner.

To be effective in compromising with your partner, you both must take a team approach in decision-making. You also must have an open mind and a willingness to accept some self-sacrifice. This is what being in a relationship is all about. It's not all just about you anymore; it's about both of you. The choices you make as a couple should include both partners; unless one allows the other to make the sole decision on a matter, such as choosing a restaurant to celebrate a special occasion.

There will be many cases when couples agree on decisions or positions, but when they don't; compromising is the logical option. But, realistically, there will be times when couples won't necessarily be able to compromise on issues—usually on matters of a serious nature. That's when relationships becomes somewhat challenged. For example, if one partner has a strong emotional position on something, the other partner for the sake of being cooperative and understanding; may reluctantly agree with their partner's decision.

The goal of compromising is to attempt to come to an agreement that meets close to a common ground. This is where communication plays an important role. Couples need to discuss their different positions honestly and determine what alternatives are available that are agreeable to them.

Again, not all decisions couples make will require compromising. Many times they have similar opinions and choices about both unimportant and important matters. It is when they differ on those matters when the art of compromising comes into play.

Also, when you are in a personal relationship, it's essential to consult with your partner before making a decision, even when the decision does not impact your partner directly.

Faithfulness

Being faithful to your partner is another important quality that your relationship must have if it is to survive. I use to watch the television show *Cheaters*. The surprising thing for me, particularly among the cheating men, was that many times they were cheating with a woman less attractive than their girlfriend or wife. Also, I was puzzled why the cheater of the relationship did not merely break the relationship off. Instead, they continued staying with their partner while cheating on the side. Either they were afraid to come clean with their partner that they no longer wanted to be with or they wanted their cake and eat it too.

Men seem to have a reputation for cheating on their partner more so than women. But women do have a history of doing a lot of cheating themselves. Why does one cheat on their partner? There are many reasons, but one of the most frequent causes is that their relationship with their partner lacks something or they have become incompatible. For example, it could be one is spending too much time away, and the relationship has become distant. Sexual fulfillment or other factors in the relationship may be lacking, causing one or both partners to cheat. And sometimes it can be a matter of couples wanting to get out of the relationship because they found someone else more appealing than their existing partner.

It's never a good situation for neither when couples are in relationships where one or both are unfaithful. This not only creates anger, mistrust, and emotional pain; but also could lead to sexual diseases as well as violence.

If you are seeking long-term relationships, including marriage; for most, your aim is to be faithful to your partner throughout the relationship. To keep your relationship healthy, you make it a priority. This means, not allowing your job, children, parents, or anyone else to cause friction in your relationship. Focus on fulfilling the basic needs of your partner, whatever those desires may be.

Of course, there are exceptions, but in most cases, consistently meeting the needs of your partner will help keep him or her from going astray.

Also, a factor that can give some assurance of faithfulness in your relationship is to strive to find someone that has morals and values. During the dating and courting process seek such qualities out. For example, ask potential partner questions about their thoughts on being faithful. You want to get their opinions on such subjects should you decide to pursue a long-term relationship with them. Other conversations concerning trust and honesty should also be discussed to determine your potential compatibility.

Honesty

Honesty among couples is essential to their relationship. When a couple cannot be honest with each other, it leads to mistrust, suspicion, and resentment. We owe it to our partner to be honest with them regardless of what the outcome will result from that honesty.

Honesty creates a foundation of trust. It is essential for cooperation and integrity in long-term relationships. Your partner will trust and respect you when you are honest and open with them; this is a natural human reaction.

Using the television show *Cheaters* again as an example, the cheating partner could have avoided trouble by before cheating, informing his or her partner that the relationship was in trouble. Perhaps then, both could have had an honest discussion on why there were relationship problems and how to fix them. Instead, the cheating partner goes out and finds someone else to fulfill whatever needs that his or her partner was not providing.

Held in high esteem in the dating environment is honesty. Yet, many people on dating sites lie on their profiles. For example, some may lie about their height and weight and cover up their deception by ensuring that the photos they post do not show their true stature and size.

Usually, few relationships can survive when one or both partners are forever dishonest with each other. On-going lying to your partner with the intent to deceive is cruel, abusive, and cowardly.

If you are on the receiving end of a relationship where your partner is habitually dishonest with you, then you may need to get out of that relationship. It will only bring you continuous emotional heartache and pain.

Make it a regular practice, to be honest with your mate. If you are in a relationship with someone that continually lies to you, then move on. That relationship is finished. Couples, whether in new or established relationships, need honesty from each other to feel secure in their partnership. Without honesty in a relationship, there is no harmony or trust.

Humor

Humor is healthy for both our mind and body. Laughter can raise our heart rate and fortify our immune system. There is an old saying; people laugh more when they are healthy, and they are healthy if they laugh more.

In your relationship with your partner, strive to find situations that spark a smile in them. It can be a simple story that has humor or a playful tickle under the arm that makes your partner laugh or smile.

One does not have to be a comedian to make his or her partner laugh or smile. Having a light-hearted nature about yourself and the ability to make the other smile is usually all it takes. Also, humor can come from looking at something in a different way that brings a smile or laughter to your mate.

People enjoy being around those that make them laugh or smile. On dating sites profiles, especially those of women, many say they are looking for someone that makes them laugh or smile. What they are essentially saying they are looking for someone that will make them happy or feel good. Humor has a way of doing that.

We all have had funny things that have happened to us. Telling such comical stories to our partner or partner-to-be would surely help put them in a good mood after a long, hard, and stressful day. Sometimes telling even embarrassing stories about yourself can bring laughter to your mate. The key is to incorporate laughter into your relationship regularly. Couples that laugh together have a better chance of their relationship lasting. Watch how your partner eyes sparkle when you make them laugh or smile. Bring humor to the lives of your partner will surely generate deposits in their Emotional Love Bank.

Whether you're at home or out on a date with your mate, make it a habit of putting a smile on your partner's face. Humor is a form of communication. You send a message to the receiver, whether verbally or physically as a result of your humor. With humor, the expected response is a smile or a laugh.

Couples should find making the other smile or laugh easy, especially after they have been together for a while and learned how to get a laugh or smile out of them.

I often tell people that couples that laugh together stay together. Happiness is when our needs are met; laughter is one of those needs. Nothing is quite as sweet as the sound of your lover breaking down into a joyful laugh as a result of something you said or did. Through laughter, you not only increased your partner's heart rate but also fortified his or her immune system. Make it a regular practice of enticing your mate to laugh or smile.

There is an old saying: You don't stop laughing because you grow old; you grow old because you stop laughing. This speaks volume on how important laughter is to our health and well being.

Yes, humor is among those must-have qualities for relationships to be successful. Don't just take my word for it. Observe many successful couples that you know and ask them how humor has sustained their happiness. I'm sure they will give you a response that will bring a smile on your face.

Kindness

Another trait that both men and women look for in loving relationships is kindness. The good thing about being kind to someone in your love life is that not a lot of effort is required. For example, telling your partner that you love them is a show of kindness. Also, giving your partner a relaxing back massage after a hard day at work is another demonstration of kindness.

When you consistently do things that make your mate feel special, you are adding deposits to their Emotional Love Bank. Your thoughtfulness also will be rewarded with kindness in return from your partner. Expressions of kindness not only brighten your mate's day, but also put them in a wonderful mood, with you on their mind.

Kind gestures mean a lot to relationships. Seek out ways to show how much you appreciate your partner by doing things that make them feel loved, happy, and grateful. Life can be hectic and stressful at times, find ways, whether they are creative or not, to bring relaxation and happiness in your relationship by doing kind and thoughtful things for your mate.

It also helps to know what makes your mate happy. This allows you to do the things that he or she will appreciate. Also, remember to say thank you to your partner when they did something for you. Showing your partner that you are grateful is a reflection of not only appreciation but also kindness.

When you show the woman or man in your life attention by being kind to them, they are more likely to feel good about themselves as well as feel good about you. Having someone in their life that is thoughtful and kind makes them feel special. The more attention you give them, the more attention you will get in return. Kindness among couples makes their relationship strong, romantic, and loving.

Likability

You can be the most beautiful woman a man has set eyes on, but if you are not likable; all that beauty will not matter, especially for men that are looking for long-term relationships. The same can be said about handsome men. Yes, many single women have desires of meeting tall and handsome men; but if they are found later to be snobby, rude, and downright mean; those same women would be turned off by them. What this all says is that likability is an essential quality women (and men) look for in a partner and good looks alone is not enough.

This does not mean physical beauty is not a factor. As we discussed earlier, physical appearance is the first thing people see of you that gets their attention. This is true on dating sites, at social events, and other places. If you capture someone's interest as a result of your good looks; they become interested in you. However, after some conversation and spending a bit of time with you to get to know your character, their impression of you can change either positively or negatively; depending on your being likable or not.

Therefore, your character, ultimately, along with other factors discussed, is what determines your likability by others. No one wants to be around someone with a bad attitude and is a hell-raiser.

When you're in a relationship, whether it's new or established, when one or both of you stop liking or respecting the other, usually that relationship will be difficult to survive. So, likability has a lot of substance in a relationship.

Just like best friends relationships among couples can outlast romantic relationships, so can likability. For example, when my ex-wife and I devoiced, we remained friends and still liked each other as individuals. So, when you are searching for that particular person that might be the love of your life, make sure that they are likable as well as lovable.

Relationships and marriages may dissolve, but if they initially based on liking the other, and that likability still exist, they can remain, platonic friends, while moving onto new personal relationships elsewhere.

Love

A lady friend of mine that I have known for quite a while, which I will call Samantha was a frequent user of online dating sites. Most of the men she dated were those she met online. Her favorite online dating sites were Christian Mingle and Plenty of Fish. Because we were good friends and talked over the phone at least two times a month, she would tell me about some of the interesting dates she had. This one guy she anxiously told me about excited her. She even claimed she was in love with him.

"Marcus, I met this nice handsome guy on Christian Mingle, and we have so much in common!" She said to me over the phone.

"That's great, Samantha!" I said genuinely happy for her because she had been looking for the right guy for such a long time.

"I really love him, Marcus," Samantha said with sincerity in her voice.

"So, how long have you been seeing him?" I asked.

"We have not met yet, but we have been talking on the phone and emailing each other three to four times a week for months," Samantha said to my surprise.

"Samantha, you mean you have yet to meet this guy in person. How can you be in love with someone you have never met?" I said in a fatherly manner.

"It's just the way I feel about him. He feels the same about me," she replied.

After some back and forth conversation about love and what it is, I suggested or demanded that Samantha keep her emotions in check about being in love with a guy she never actually met yet. I also told her she must meet the guy before getting too much emotionally involved with him. I also warned her to make sure he's not a scammer and that the photo in the profile is really him.

Months later, my friend was heartbroken when she finally discovered the guy she believed to have fallen in love with was a scammer. She appropriately cut off all interactions with the guy.

My friend thought she was in love with someone that she had never met. On-going conversations with a smooth-talking stranger had stolen her heart and now broken it by being a scammer and lying to her. He had made her believe he was also in love with her. I cannot tell you how emotionally hurt she was after she had learned the man she thought she was in love with was a scammer. Many women, as well as men on dating sites, are subject to fall for such tricks. Sometimes it's a result of being lonely and wanting so badly to find love. When someone does give them the attention, admiration, and conversation that they have been lacking, they almost become like putty in the hands of the person that shows them such false admiration.

True love is quite different. It takes time. Before you genuinely fall in love with someone, you spend lots of time getting to know them. You develop a likeness for that person, and when you're not together, you either talk to each other over the phone. Or you may email or text each other and make plans for spending time together.

Love requires spending time with each other to learn everything possible about one another. It means sharing laughter and stories about your past and present that allows the person that you have grown to like, to know you, and like you as well. Love also means to show your feelings by touching that the person. Love is also about being honest and sincere to each other while building trust. Love is also being able to confide and talk about anything with the person, knowing that it brings you closer together as friends and someone you can share anything about yourself. Love means doing things with that person, knowing that it will make them as happy as you are.

My friend, Samantha, is now more cautious with the men she meets online. I hope that she finds the right man for her because she is a good person, and deserve to be loved in return by someone compatible with her.

As I told Samantha, true love takes time, and putting in the time to build a loving relationship is worth it.

Reliability

When you are in a healthy relationship, you rely on each other as a couple to do the things that you promised to do. You also rely on each other to help when it's needed, whether it's something as trivial as taking out the trash or more serious as coming to each other's aid should one of you get arrested for whatever reason.

A cousin of mine, I'll call Delilah, got divorced in 2017 after five years of marriage discussed with me while at our family reunion why she ended her marriage.

"Marcus, I could hardly ever depend on Sonny (not his real name) for help with raising the children, fixing things around the house, or just being a good husband," Delilah said with frustration in her voice as we talked in a secluded area of the hotel lobby where our family reunion was being held.

"Well, did he show such unreliable characteristics when you were dating, and if so, why did you marry him?" I asked.

"No, he was very dependable during the seven months that we were dating. If I needed him for something, he was there in a heartbeat," Delilah said.

I then asked Delilah had she talked to him to try to find out what was causing him to change. She said they had many discussions about his behavior changes, but he was evasive and avoided talking much about it.

After I did some additional probing, Delilah embarrassingly admitted that Sonny had been cheating on her. That's when I realized what possibly contributed to his changing from someone reliable to undependable.

Although my cousin did not initially want to admit to me, it was not only her husband unreliability that contributed to her devoicing him, but probably more so his infidelity.

Since that conversation with Delilah, she is happily in a new relationship. Although marriage is not in the picture, she is living with someone that is both reliable and faithful.

Most men and women seeking long-term relationships want the comfort of knowing their mate can be depended upon—not just for small matters, but also the important things. For example, should you get sick; you want to have peace of mind in knowing that you can depend on your partner to run errands for you or take care of you until you are feeling better.

When you're in a relationship, your partner is also expected to be able to depend on you. Couples that live in the same household are supposed to share cleaning, cooking, babysitting, and other domestic duties around the house. You both are a team, and teammates share in responsibilities.

Respect

A loving relationship cannot survive without both partners treating each other with respect. Respect bonds relationships. From the way you communicate to the actions you make with each other, respect must permeate in the relationship.

The key to healthy relationships is respect. This does not mean there won't be periods when you become angry with your partner and have shouting matches as a result of disagreements. Some, if not many relationships, whether they're married or not, do from time to time, have such drama. But, after letting off some steam and later apologizing, couples must return to giving each other the proper respect that all loving relationships should have.

Practically, all couples from time to time have bad days and get into arguments. But good relationships and marriages do it respectfully. Meaning, avoiding name-calling and intentionally saying things that you know would emotionally hurt your partner.

Being respectful of each other is paramount for relationships to last. What are the ways we can show respect to our mate? This list is a sample:

- Be a good listener, giving your undivided attention
- Keep your promises; do the things you said you would do
- Offer help without being asked
- Know when to give him or her their space
- Apologize when you did something wrong, and do it quickly
- When your mate is stressed over something, provide them with a hug and kiss
- Keep the noise down when your partner is sleeping or not feeling well
- Tell your mate how much you love them
- Be understanding, compassionate, and available.
- Be around not only during happy times but also during crises.

When you show such respectable behaviors, you demonstrate how much you admire, love, and value your partner. Couples that treat each other with respect and kindness have a strong foundation for a loving and happy relationship. Remember to get respect; you must be willing to give respect.

Romance

Romance is an important quality for a successful relationship between couples. It helps to keep the relationship fresh and stimulating while also creating a mood and an expression of love and care.

When we show affection to our mate, we can also create a romantic mood. For example, one of the most beautiful things an ex-girlfriend did for me out of nowhere while we were talking was removed my shoes and socks and started giving me a slow and relaxing foot massage. This blew my mind! At the time, I was in my early 30s, and I had never had a girlfriend do this to me before. Not only was it relaxing, but also romantic. She, out of nowhere, created a romantic mood as a result of showing her affection toward me by giving me a soothing foot massage. Of course, that massage led to another thing, but I digress. After a year of dating, we eventually broke up, but she forever made an impression on me with those wonderful foot massages.

There are several other ways couples can be romantic. Among them could include going out for dinner, followed by an evening of dancing. Also, sending your partner a hand-written love letter can be romantic. Writing love letters has become a lost art in the act of courtship.

What couples get out of romance is what they put into it. Romance satisfies our need for overt demonstration of love. We feel reassured when someone's love for us is displayed. It increases the senses of our worth. It heightens our sense of identity of being unique and a desirable person. It can reassure women they are beautiful and desirable as well as confirm to men they are handsome and needed.

Everyone in a relationship needs a demonstration from their partner's awareness and appreciation of them. No one wants to be taken for granted.

Without providing romance in your relationship, there is a tendency of your mate feeling isolated.

Learn to take advantage of those special days such as Valentine's Day, birthdays, and other occasions to do something special and creative with your partner that will generate a romantic atmosphere. Go on vacations together, including places where both of you have never been.

Keeping the romance alive in your relationship requires being aware of your partner's emotional and physical needs and knowing how to meet those needs. This helps to further build a foundation of pleasure and contentment in your relationship.

To create and keep the romance alive in your relationship with your partner takes a show of tender loving care and a desire to want to please and show your mate how much they mean to you.

Sex

First, let me state that many long-term relationships are successful without sexual intercourse. For example, some couples, due to health or disability reasons, cannot have sex; therefore, they find alternate ways of being intimate. Others couples have long-term relationships with no sexual activities by choice alone.

However, for many healthy men and women in a long-term relationship, sexual intercourse is a key factor in their relationship. If they are going to have a long-term healthy relationship, the sex must be part of the equation.

Although there are exceptions, sex is just as important to women as it is to men. Society has portrayed men as having a strong appetite for sex, and I can't deny that point. However, women also have a strong desire for sex, but generally hide it better than men. When ladies get together for a girls night out and other gatherings, I can assure you they are not just talking about their cooking recipes, issues with the kids, or what they are going to wear at the next New Year's Eve party. Sex will pop up in women conversation, eventually.

However, women on dating sites that are looking for long-term relationships sometimes make it clear to those reading their profile that they are looking for a stable relationship. They may state in their profile to those men that have sex only on their mind something such as: "If you're looking for only sex or a one-night stand, keep it moving, I'm not that type of woman."

Also, for both women and men, when going out on dates whether with someone you met online or offline; get to know the person before engaging in sex. There are too many sexual diseases out there; some can also kill you. Avoid having hasty sex with someone you just met. If they are someone that you feel is a good match for you, first, get to know them better by spending time with them. It takes at least six or seven months to get to know someone, and sometimes it takes at least a year. Is that too long before having sex with them? For some couples, maybe so. But if you still don't know them well, and question their honesty; waiting longer is worth it. The bottom line: never have sex with someone that you know little about or don't trust. This is common sense.

Again, dating is about getting to know each other while spending adequate time with each other to determine whether you are both a good fit. Dating is a time to ask each other lots of questions, including at some point having honest discussions about sex. The proper time to ask such types of questions is after you had a few dates and are comfortable with each other.

When you are in an established relationship, learn how to please each other sexually. This comes from communicating honestly about what pleases each other and even experimenting with different sexual positions. Sex should be fun and a way of demonstrating your love and passion for your partner. It is also healthy, emotionally bonding and acts as a relaxer of relationships when life gets stressful. Sex is also a way to solidify your closeness with your partner.

If you and your mate need energy and variety in your sex life, here are some things you may want to incorporate in your lovemaking repertoire:

- Give each other a half an hour or hour full body massage. Also, wear something sexy while you are giving and receiving the massage.

- Have sex in a different area of your home or apartment, such as in the shower. Also, make love to varying times of the day.
- Expand your sexual knowledge by reading books and watch informational videos. Talk openly with your partner what you learned and include it in your sex life for adding variety and excitement.
- Do the things that turn your mate on while continuing to explore new ways to increase you and your partner sexual enjoyment.

Time

Relationships do not work by themselves. Couples need to create a bond and nurture their relationship. This is done by spending lots of time with each other.

When I was a younger man in my early twenties, I dated several women and some I liked more than others. However, I was not committed to any of them, and I demonstrated this by the limited amount of time I spent with them. For example, not only did I visit them about once a week but I also only phoned them about twice a week. This was not the way to develop a relationship with a person that you desire. After work, I would play basketball or tennis in the evening, and later, if I were in the mood, I would phone my lady friend to chat. How I spent my time, or lack of time, showed I was not, at least mentally, ready for a relationship. I knew it, and so did the women I call myself dating realize it.

I eventually learned that giving proper time to a relationship is essential to its success. When I met my future wife and realized how special she was, I started to put in the time to learn more about her. We frequently talked over the phone. I visited her home and met her parents and other relatives. I was not going to make the mistakes I had made with the other women I had dated.

Making your relationship work with your better half should be a priority. This means everything else is secondary other than your relationship with God.

Whether you meet someone new or if you are already in an established relationship; you must spend time with each other to allow the relationship to grow strong. Human beings tend to bond together as they interact with each other. This is especially true in relationships.   As I said before, women particularly need such bonding and time with their partner to feel secure and close to their mate.

If you are dating someone and not living in the same household with them, you both should have some interaction with each other daily. Whether it's through phone conversations, texting, actual visits, or other means of contact; regular communication will help make your relationship close, meaningful, and secure. Your love for each other will become stronger as a result of you spending time together and interacting with each other. Should you miss a day without any interaction with each other, you're probably feel somewhat guilty about it because it will be a rare occasion.

Avoid taking your relationship for granted. You could come face to face with losing it as a result of not giving it the proper time and attention required in making it run smoothly. Time makes no promises; it will not wait for you; therefore, put in the time for your relationships while you can.

Time is precious, and spending lots of it with the person who is the love of our life is worth it. Regardless of the type of work you do, other outside commitments you have; make sure that ample time is positively devoted to your partner. This will not only help you keep deposits in their Emotional Love Bank, but also keep your loving partnership strong and healthy.

Trust

Last, but surely not least, trust is essential for a relationship between a man and woman to survive. Just like honesty, if your relationship lacks trust, it is already on life support. When you and your partner have complete trust in each other, you can depend on one another. You have total faith in each other, and this, in turn, gives your relationship security.

Trust in a relationship occurs when couples are open to each other about their thoughts and feelings. Discuss concerns and feelings about matters openly. Give your mate the confidence and comfort in knowing that he or she can discuss anything in confidence with you. For those in new relationships or relationships where trust has been questioned, developing trust may take some time. For example, if you have given your partner reasons not to trust you, that trust would have to be regained over time. Trust is essential to a happy relationship.

I had a friend named Jimmy, whose wife, Cindy had lost trust in him because he had cheated on her during their first year of marriage. One day he came home late from work and his wife became suspicious of him; wondering if he was still being unfaithful to her. Jimmy honestly told Cindy that he was late because he had been stuck in traffic due to an unfortunate accident. Cindy doubted him, but when she heard the news on television that reported on the traffic accident which included one fatality; she realized Jimmy was telling the truth. Cindy quickly apologized to him, realizing that she still needed some time for her trust in Jimmy to be restored. In due time, Cindy later began trusting Jimmy again, and I'm happy to say the couple is still married and doing well.

Trust will always be among those key factors that maintain a healthy relationship among couples. If for some reason you and your partner lose trust in each other, work extra hard to restore it.

Whether your relationships are personal, professional, or otherwise, you will have to prove your trustworthiness to others, especially when people don't quite know you. In such cases, trust is established over time. For example, in the workplace, when you're new on the job, your boss gain confidence in your work based on the results of your work performance. If you consistently do a great job, you gained his confidence and trust in your abilities to handle the job successfully. The same is true in a new loving relationship. As your relationship grows and your partner gains trust in you based upon a pattern of reliability, truthfulness, and other positive behaviors that builds confidence in a relationship.

When you are developing a new relationship in the dating world, maintain consistency in what you say and do so that you build trust in your new partner. Be open to them in talking about the tough topics. Be honest about your thoughts and feelings. Trust in new relationships can take time; your goal is to prove your trustworthiness to your partner.

When I lived and worked in Indianapolis back in the late 70s, I worked hard in making my new girlfriend, Bernice, trust me. During the early stages of our relationship, I could tell that she was somewhat cautious of me, given that I had picked her up off the street in the rain while she was waiting for a bus. It would not have surprised me that earlier in our relationship that she wondered did I make a habit of picking up women on the street. When she finally did ask me how often I have picked up a distressed woman in the street, I told her she was the first. I was honest with her whether she believed me or not. She was indirectly trying to figure if I was trustworthy. It took her some time to trust me because our relationship was new, and we were both still learning about each other. We both had to gain trust in each other over time.

Trust, especially in a new relationship, has to be built over time. It must be earned and established as a result of being honest and open with your partner and consistent in your interaction and behavior with your mate.

Key Points to Remember or Act Upon

- Swarm your lover with affection will make your relationship exciting, healthy, and romantic. The wonderful thing about showing affection is that it does not have to be something that cost you money. A simple kiss, backrub, or even kind words in an email message, are all ways to show your partner you care about them.
- If you and your partner can not honestly say you are best friends, make a strong effort to nurture your relationship so that you grow into becoming best friends. I can guarantee that you won't regret it!
- It's always best to be in a relationship with someone that shares your interests, tastes, and values. Not only will you be happier in such a relationship, but the percentage of such a partnership lasting is much higher as opposed one who has significant different interests and values.
- Nothing is quite as sweet as the sound of your lover breaking down into a joyful laugh as a result of something you said or did. Through laughter, you not only increased your partner's heart rate but also fortified his or her immune system. Make it a regular practice of enticing your mate to laugh or smile.
- Time is precious, and spending lots of it with the person who is the love of our life is worth it. Regardless of the type of work you do, other outside commitments you have; make sure that ample time is positively devoted to your partner.

Chapter 16

To Enhance Your Relationship Increase Emotional Love Bank Deposits

We all have Emotional Love Bank Accounts, whether we realize it or not. But before I get ahead of myself, let me first explain what it is. In its simplest terms, an Emotional Love Bank Account is a metaphor that illustrates how we affect each other emotionally in practically every interaction we have with each other. Those interactions are referred to as deposits or withdrawals. Those deposits and withdrawals result in the amount or lack of trust, comfort, and secure experience that has been built up in a relationship. Throughout your interactions with each other, you may make deposits, which are considered positive interactions; and withdrawals, which are considered negative interactions.

Our Emotional Love Bank is always figuratively opened for those we interact with to make these on-going deposits and withdrawals. Our Emotional Love Bank contains many different accounts for people we interact with whether they are relatives, friends, co-workers, and others we associate with in some way or another. However, for this chapter, we are going to address the Emotional Love Bank as it relates to someone we are dating or in a long-term relationship.

The Sandra and Sonny Story

To show how this concept works in a typical new dating situation, let's take a make-believe couple named Sandra and Sonny. The couple met on a dating site and exchanged pleasant greetings followed by warm conversations that led to them emailing each other off the dating site. Through these communications, they were making deposits in each other Emotional Love Bank, whether they realized it or not. Days later, they finally exchanged phone numbers and were having extensive phone conversations that led them anxiously looking forward to their first date.

When Sandra and Sonny had their first date at a coffee shop, they could not keep their eyes off each other. Both thought that each looked even better than their online profile photos. Sonny, to Sandra surprise, also gave her a bouquet. As a result, he just made a significant deposit to Sandra's Emotional Love Bank. Sandra returned the favor by telling Sonny how much she admires his generosity and gentlemen behavior.

Before long, Sandra and Sonny were seeing each other more frequently, at least three to four times a week. The couple relationship was going so well they even decided to take a weekend get-way trip together. Driving from Indianapolis to Wisconsin Dells meant that the couple would be spending more extended time together for the first time. This allowed them to learn more about each other in a different environment while also putting their still early relation to somewhat of a test.

When the couple arrived at the lodge house they shared, Sandra noticed that Sonny threw his clothes around the bedroom without hanging them up inside the closet. He also made a mess of the bathroom they shared; leaving the top off the toothpaste and water all over the sink. Sandra begins to realize that Sonny was a slob. His lousy housekeeping manners had induced withdrawals from Sandra's Emotional Love Bank. Sandra began to complain to Sonny about his sloppiness and asked that he try to be a bit neater.

Sonny took Sandra complaints as a form of nagging, and as a result, she made withdrawals from his Emotional Love Bank.

By evening, the couple went boating together and sightseeing, regenerating new deposits in their Emotional Love Banks, despite the earlier withdrawals of the day.

The following day, the last day of their get-away weekend trip, the couple engaged in arguments over how they wanted to spend the day. They also began to have second thoughts about their relationship. The couple's Emotional Love Bank withdrawals had increased to the level that they could not wait to end their trip. They were anxious to return to their separate homes to re-evaluate whether the relationship should continue.

The time spent together on their trip taught the couple they had some issues that needed resolving between them if they were to salvage their relationship. Although many of their complaints with one another were not that serious, for them, they were issues that affected their relationship emotionally. Although each Emotional Love Bank still had plenty of deposits, the magnitude of the negative withdrawals seemed to outweigh the positive deposits.

Sandra and Sonny still had more deposits than withdrawals in their Emotional Love Bank, which indicated their relationship still had a strong possibility of surviving. However, positive deposits from both would need to continue to grow in each other's Emotional Love Bank if their relationship were to survive.

Make More Deposits to Your Long-term Relationship

The lesson learned from Sandra and Sonny story is to make more deposits to one's Emotional Love Bank and try to work through the withdrawals.

Whether you are at the early stages of your relationship or already in a long-term relationship, there must be on-going deposits made to each other's Emotional Love Bank for there to be consistent happiness, comfort, and emotional prosperity. Continuous deposits help to secure and sustain a relationship. There are also many types of deposits you can make to your partner's Emotional Love Bank. But again, those deposits must be constant.

To know what types of deposits to make to your long-term relationship with someone, you must understand that person. When you know what gives a person you care about joy, comfort, affection, and other feelings of delight; you are better equipped with what constitutes a deposit for your partner. Therefore, get to know what makes your partner feel happy and safe. Understand what helps build trust and reassurance in your partner.

The accumulation of both positive and negative experience affects our emotional reaction to those which we receive those positive deposits and negative withdrawals. The more deposits we receive from a person in our Emotional Love Bank, the more positive emotional reaction we have with that person.   While the more withdrawals made by a person to our Emotional Love Bank, the more negative emotional response we have with that person.

The Different Levels of Deposits and Withdrawals we make to One's Emotional Love Bank

The level or degree of deposits and withdrawals also play a critical role in our Emotional Love Bank. Just as we make different levels of deposits and withdrawals in our financial banking institutions, we also produce different levels of deposits and withdrawals to each others' Emotional Love Bank. There are small deposits and withdrawals; medium deposits and withdrawals; and large deposits and withdrawals.

Here are examples of the different levels of positive deposits a married man makes to his wife Emotional Love Bank: After coming home from work the husband goes directly to his wife and plants a soft kiss on her cheek, telling her he loves her; this generally represents a small deposit. Later in the day, he gives her a rare relaxing foot massage; that's a medium deposit. The next day, he surprises her with a five-day trip to the Bahamas for both of them; that's an example of a larger deposit.

The different levels of withdrawals work in the same manner but only in a negative nature. Let's use an example of a couple that's been dating for a while. The girlfriend breaks the date with her boyfriend giving little explanation of why except that she does not feel like going out and wants some time alone. This would generally rank as a small withdrawal to her boy friend's Emotional Love Bank. A couple of days later, the girlfriend tells her boyfriend that she needs some space and suggest that they do not see each other for at least a week; therefore making a medium withdrawal. After a week of the couple not seeing each other, the boyfriend walks through a park and notice his girlfriend snuggled up with a strange guy on a park bench. For the boyfriend, this is a large withdrawal to his Emotional Love Bank.

It should be noted that the levels of deposits and withdrawals can vary and be subjective, depending on how the person emotionally receive or interpret those deposits and withdrawals.

As with the example of Sandra and Sonny; major withdrawals can sometimes trump one's Emotional Love Bank filled with more deposits than withdrawals. For example, a wife received more deposits in her Emotional Love Bank from her husband, but if he often physically beats her, those reserve of deposits may mean less given the serious nature of beatings she received from him. Therefore, the different levels of deposits and withdrawals can play a big part in one's Emotional Love Bank.

Still, for relationships to remain strong, couples need to make more deposits to each other's Emotional Love Bank. Other types of deposits to ensure success in a relationship includes being respectful to your partner; doing things with your partner you don't necessarily like to do, but you know it will make them happy, so you do them anyway; and keeping commitments and promises that you made. These are examples of actions and behaviors that build up your deposits in your partner's Emotional Love Bank and ultimately improve and heighten your relationship; regardless if it's a new relationship or an already established relationship.

Inevitably, there will be times withdrawals will be made to your loved one's Emotional Love Bank. The key is to keep them at a minimum and lowest level type of withdrawals. When they become major withdrawals, they put your relationship at risk, especially if they are repeated.

Also, apologize to your partner when you realize you made obvious withdrawals to his or her Emotional Love Bank. Make sure the apology is sincere.

During the initial stages of dating, understand the Emotional Love Bank concept. Put in more deposits than withdrawals in the Emotional Love Bank of the person you are dating and watch how the relationship successfully grows. When you maintain a high reserve of deposits in your partner's Emotional Love Bank, they usually reciprocate. Therefore, focus on being kind, thoughtful, honest, faithful, and giving in your relationship. This is very important if you both are intending to have a loving long-term relationship.

As for that first date, when you tell that person, "Thank you for a wonderful evening," whether you realize it or not; you just made a deposit to their Emotional Love Bank.

Key Points to Remember or Act Upon

- An Emotional Love Bank Account is a metaphor that illustrates how we affect each other emotionally with practically every interaction we have with each other. Those interactions are referred to as deposits or withdrawals.
- Whether you are at the early stages of your dating relationship or already in a long-term relationship, for it to bring happiness, comfort, and emotional prosperity; there must be on-going deposits made to your partner's Emotional Love Bank.
- The level of deposits and withdrawals also play a critical role in our Emotional Love Bank. Just as we make different levels of deposits and withdrawals in our financial banking institutions, we also make different levels of deposits and withdrawals in each others' Emotional Love Bank.
- Put in more deposits than withdrawals in the Emotional Love Bank of the person you are dating and watch how the relations successfully grow. When you maintain a high reserve of deposits in your partner's Emotional Love Bank, they usually can't help themselves from reciprocating.

Chapter 17

Factors That Make Long-Distance Relationships Successful

When I lived in Indianapolis, Indiana, during the late 1970s, I dated a woman eight years older than me. During those days, there were no online dating sites. I met her on a rainy afternoon while driving to the store on a Saturday. She was standing in the rain near a bus stop without an umbrella. The woman was looking gorgeous, despite being in distress because of the ongoing rain and the bus being nowhere in sight. Being a gentleman, I slowly drove my car up to her, making sure not to splash her with any rain water on the ground. Then I rolled down my window, and offered to drive her to wherever she was going. She smiled politely while carefully looking me over. I'm sure it was to ensure I didn't look like a rapist or other type of criminal. Afterward, she graciously got into my car; relieved to have gotten out of the rain. We had a pleasant conversation as I drove her home. Bernice (not her real name), had been shopping and forgotten to take an umbrella. When I arrived at her apartment, she thanked me for getting her out of the rain and driving her home. She then, to my surprise, gave me her phone number and asked that I call her soon. I did, and the rest was history.

Bernice and I remained a couple during my last two years in Indianapolis. When I quit my job and decided to move back to my hometown, Chicago, I didn't consider taking Bernice with me. Primarily because she had four children that range in ages 8 to 17, and it would be an inconvenience to uproot them from their schools they enjoyed attending. Therefore, I suggested to Bernice that I would visit her once a month. Besides, Indianapolis was roughly about a three-hour drive, and I was a young man with a nice dependable car.

However, after three months, those once a month, three-hour trips began to take a toll on me both physically and mentally. Also, being in two different cities had made us somewhat distance more than just in terms of miles but also relationship-wise. Neither of us had been in a long-distance relationship before; this was a new lifestyle for us. Although we had regular phone conversations about four or five times a week, not being physically there for each other had negatively affected our relationship. Eventually, Bernice and I broke up; we realized that long-distance relationships were not for us.

The Complexity of Long-Distance Relationships

Some people are in long-distance relationships for many reasons. One partner may be in the armed service, working in another distance city for a certain period, or various other reasons. Many of these types of long-distance relationships are usually temporary and the couples typically know each other rather well. However, when dating someone new and trying to establish a relationship with them from several miles away; it can be extra challenging as compared to couples that already know each other well.

Therefore, when searching for a compatible mate on a dating site and you come across someone that captures your eye that lives very far, ask yourself some serious questions before reaching out to them. The three initial questions you need to ask yourself include:

1. Are you capable and willing to make a commitment to a long-distance relationship?
2. Are you willing to make the necessary sacrifices for the relationship to work?
3. What is the maximum amount of time you are willing to stay in the long-distance arrangement before deciding to move in together or closer or end the relationship?

The first two questions require a simple yes or no, and you don't necessarily have to know the person on the dating site that captured your interest. These two questions help determine if you are capable of being in a long-distance relationship, regardless of who the person is of interest. If you can honestly answer yes to both questions, then you potentially have the right attitude for being in a long-distance relationship. Therefore, you can proceed with giving that person that lives 400 miles away on the dating site an introductory greeting that hopefully generates a pleasant response.

However, question number three also requires an honest answer. The purpose of that question is to determine how long you are willing to put up with a long-distance arrangement. Of course, the other person would have some say about it. But you still should have some idea when you are willing to end the long-distance arrangement. That could mean moving in together, living closer, or ending the relationship.

Establish a Time Limit for Your Long-Distance Relationship

Although Bernice and I had given the long-distance arrangement a try, we later found out we were lousy at it. Had the technology that is available today for communicating long-distance been around back then, perhaps our relationship would have survived. Back in the late 70s, video communication tools and services such as Skype were not around nor was the Internet. However, thanks to today's advanced communication technology, many people have successful long-distance relationships. But it takes more than technology to help long-distance relationships to survive.

Of the friends and strangers that I have spoken with that have made their long-distance relationship work, many of them seem to say similar things about what makes such relationships successful.

A key factor they say is critical when going into a long-distance relationship is to create a realistic time limit that you both are willing to commit to the long-distance lifestyle.

Many surveys show that most people do not wish to have a long-distance relationship with someone they are dating or in an established relationship. But if it's going be a temporary thing, some are willing to give it a try provided that there is a reasonable time limit. When that time limit ends, both are expected to live closer to each other, whether in the same house or nearby. However, if for example, you meet someone online who lives very far and you begin to develop a relationship with them, but find out later they have no desire to end your long-distance arrangement; that is a sign that you need to move on.

Show me a person that prefers a long-distance relationship with no end in sight, and I'll show you a person that have relationship closeness issues. Rarely can a couple's relationships succeed when they are apart for extended lengths of time or indefinitely. We're talking about loving relationships, not ones of convenience.

Plan Scheduled Get-Together Dates

All long-distance relationship arrangements require some face-time if it's to survive. Schedule physical visits so that both parties can enjoy each other while also strengthening and bringing reassurance to the relationship.

During scheduled visits, put your routine activities aside and devote much of your valuable time with each other. Whether the planned visits are once a month, every four weeks, or several times a year; the arrangement is up to the couple. The important thing is that the couple agrees to the get-together date arrangement and stick with it unless there is a real emergency that causes them to cancel.

When Bernice and I were living in two different cities, we, unfortunately, had no scheduled plan for our get-together dates except an occasional visit during the holidays, but not necessarily all holidays. We also visited each other on our birthdays. These were somewhat scheduled get-together dates, but sometimes we canceled due to other things getting in the way that were not really emergencies. This is what happens when you are not committed to a long-distance relationship arrangement.

The bottom line, few long-distance relationships can survive when there are not enough face-time visits planned where you both can spend quality and productive time enjoying each other's company. Such times together are special. Not only because they are rare, but also because they help rejuvenate your relationship. It provides the partnership the energy needed to prosper.

Also, when scheduling visits, make sure, if possible, that one person is not doing all the traveling to make those visits happen. Arrangements with one partner doing the bulk of the traveling put too much pressure on them. This could lead to that person tired upon arrival, stressful, moody, and even sometimes becoming ill. Therefore, indicate when and who will travel on the scheduled dates of your time together. This does not necessarily mean you have to divide the travel schedule in half, just make sure one person is not carrying the majority load of the travel visits. So, set some reasonable travel schedules which you will visit each other and adhere to them so you can enjoy spending valuable times developing your relationship.

Also, when visiting one another, don't spend all your time cooped up in the apartment or house. Go out somewhere and enjoy yourselves. This is your rare time together. Therefore, spend time doing things like going to a sporting event, restaurant, movie, play, comedy show, or whatever else that pleases you. Enjoying each other's company in different surroundings further allows you to learn more about each other. Take part in new activities that will enable you both to grow together as a couple. Make your regular visits together such a wonderful time that you can't wait for the next visit.

Communicate Often via Phone, Email, Text, Video Calls, and Regular Mail

As indicated earlier, technology has made those in long-distance relationships lives much more bearable. Such technology as video chatting, texting, and emailing has helped bridge the distance gap of those in relationships in two far-away places.

Many of the experts on the subject of long-distance relationships seem to say that it's vital for couples to communicate daily. They say daily interaction with your distance lover is essential. Of course, that interaction means communicating with each other via phone, email, texting, regular mail, and video conferencing is a must. All such tools are useful in a combination way in couple's efforts to stay in touch with each other.

I would agree that daily communications are crucial to making a long-distance relationship work. Also, the use of various forms of communication can not only add variety to the communication process but also help control costs. For example, daily long-distance phone calls can eventually add up, even when the two of you are taking alternative days in calling each other. Mixing those regular communications with email, text, and video calls such as Skype helps to keep the long-distance phone bill down. Also, as mentioned earlier, don't forget to utilize the U.S. mail by writing to each other with an old fashion love letter. Surprise each other periodically with handwritten lover letters. Giving and receiving such form of communications is a lost art in the act of courtship. Such type of written communication is more personalized and romantic than texting or emailing. The more creative you are in your communications with each other, the better.

Why are regular communications so critical? Well, without frequent conversations with your partner that you don't have physically contact with, you tend to lose that connection with them. It's what happened to Bernice and me when we attempted to maintain a long-distance relationship. We gradually stopped calling each other more frequently, and we slowly became more distance in our fragile relationship.

So, regular communications is a way to successfully learn more about each while also maintaining a link with each other. When you talk with your lover every day, you become more close to each other. You also enhance the security of your relationship and help prevent from becoming alienated from each other as a result of not seeing one another regularly.

For most women, communication is especially important. A woman's conversation with her man blends with affection. It helps her feel united with him. She feels bonded with her man, especially when he communicates with her daily. Therefore, when you are in a long-distance relationship, it's vitally important to have frequent communications if that relationship is going to grow and become successful. Because you are not living with each other and seeing one another regularly, you must frequently utilize technology to make up for the time the both of you cannot be in each other's arms.

When communicating with each other, give one another your undivided attention. This mean, avoid watching television or other activity that can be distracting in your conversation. Stay focus on each other regardless if you're talking on the phone, video chatting, texting, or other means of communicating from a distance. This is your special time of the day when you connect from afar. Therefore, give each other your full attention and talk about your day, hopes and dreams, past and future, and anything else that helps you learn more about each other and show how you care for one another. Through your communications, get to know each other's motivations in life. Learn about what makes your partner happy, sad, and angry. If you are at the early stages of your relationship, don't be afraid to talk about tough or sensitive topics such as politics and religion. When your relationship is new, you are at a growth period in your relationship; you both want to know as much about each other as possible.

Other Factors to Consider When in a Long-Distance Relationship

I would be remised if I didn't mention the other types of challenges that you may encounter while in a long-distance relationship. Among those are loneliness, temptation, guilt, regrets, sexual frustration, and possibly other harmful related thoughts. If you do from time-to-time experience such feelings, share them with your long-distance partner. Like any relationship, it's essential to share your honest opinions and thoughts with your partner. Many times in doing so, it can bring on relief from stress; provide reassurance in your relationship; and help remove some of those negative thoughts and feelings. The more you talk over things with your mate and reveal you're true feelings, the closer you usually become as a couple.

Long-distance relationships are very challenging. You and your partner need to have the attitude and commitment for such a relationship. You both must also have an agreed decision on when you plan to move out of such an arrangement to a life in which you are both physically and emotionally closer together. When such change occurs, you and your mate will realize that your long-distance relationship was well worth it.

Key Points to Remember or Act Upon

- A key factor when going into a long-distance relationship is to create a realistic time limit that you both are willing to commit to the long-distance lifestyle.
- All long-distance relationship arrangements require some face-time if it's going to survive.
- Technology has made those in long-distance relationships lives much more bearable. Such media as video chatting, texting, and emailing has helped bridge the distance gap of those in relationships in two far-away places.
- When you are in a long-distance relationship, it's vitally important to have frequent communications if that relationship is going to be successful.
- Long-distance relationships are very challenging. You and your partner need to have the attitude and commitment for such a relationship. You both must also have a plan on when to move out of the long-distance arrangement to a life in which you are both physically closer together.

Chapter 18

Making a Relationship Work While Shacking Up

Several months have passed, and you have been dating someone that you like. So much so, that you both are seriously considering moving in together. There have been discussions about marriage, but you both would first like to give that live-together a trial run.

However, like marriage, moving in together is a big step in the growth of your relationship. You're going to see each other often than you ever did before. That means also observing the realities of the different moods you're going to be in as you go through your daily lives together. You may think that you already knew so much about each other, but wait until you live together. You're going to learn even more about one another and sometimes more than you like to discover about each other. For example, there will be various quirks that you have to put up with about one another, such as one partner clipping their toenails all over the floor and not cleaning them up. Or there may be a habit of the other partner making a mess in the bathroom; with water all over the sink and floor and doing a half-way job of drying things up. These are the realities of cohabitating or shacking up – dealing with your partner's bad habits.

Some couples go into cohabitation without discussing the implications and expectations for the future. But they love each other and are willing to take the good with the bad as they come about. However, when the bad outweighs the good, complications occur.

There have been various surveys about couples living together and the outcome of those relationships after a period of cohabitation. Some of the significant issues among many of these surveys were bathroom issues followed by closet space. For example, the toilet seat ranked as the primary cause of complaints by women. At least one study said nearly 80 percent of women had issues with men leaving the toilet seat up. Men highest gripe was about the surplus of toilet paper the women they lived with used.

These and more are among grievances that couples living together must deal with when cohabitating. However, it's all about learning to adjust your behavior so that you and your partner can keep peace and tranquility in the place you call home.

When you have lived alone for a while, you sometimes are not aware of how some of your behavior can be annoying to others. Couples need to have serious discussions over the issues they have with each other. Whether its sloppiness, lousy eating habits, or recklessness; such behaviors that bother your partner needs to be addressed along with solutions to resolve them. To ignore annoying behavioral issues could eventually add additional stress to the relationship and even possibly cause a breakup.

How to Live in Harmony in the Same Household despite Your Differences

Let's face it; it's not easy for us to change our ways and habits overnight, it takes time; even when we give it our best effort. But through time and patience, changing your behavior that's irritable to your partner can occur.

Many times couples already are aware of their partner's quirks or annoying behaviors before they decide to shack up together. Many couples still move in together, thinking they will be able to change their partner's behavior once they are living under the same roof. However, both must be willing to want to change. Also, both must acknowledge that change will take some time; especially if those unpleasant behaviors have been with them for quite a while.

When you are really in love with someone, you take the good and the bad. You acknowledge that everyone has some flaws and try to learn to live with your partner's poor habits provided they are not outrageous or disgusting.

For example, good hygiene is high on the list of behaviors we value with our partner. Therefore, one should make it a priority to keep themselves and their living space clean. It's okay to miss a shower now and then, but don't make it a regular habit. The same is true to keep your living space clean. When one partner is slacking off on his or her housekeeping chores, the other partner has a right to say something.

However, whether it something as serious as a lack of proper hygiene or something as minor as burping; couples should discuss with each other about those habits that make them uncomfortable or irritable. Ignoring a partner's behavior or bad habit that turns the other off, only adds growing stress to the relationship. In a non-confrontational way, the partner that is unhappy with the conduct should at the appropriate time bring the subject up for discussion.

Let's say the lady of the house; Lisa is annoyed by her boyfriend Thad habit of talking with a mouth full of food, causing crumbs to spit out on the table. This would be the appropriate time that she should bring the subject up. She may, for example, say something like this:

"Thad, sweetie, can you please try to avoid talking with your mouth full of food. You frequently tend to spit food all over the table, and sometimes on me. It's very annoying to me. Also, sweetie, it can be embarrassing when you do the same whenever we eat out at restaurants and with friends."

Such a request by Lisa is non-confrontational and politely states how the bad behavior by Thad makes her feel. Nor did it sound as though she was nagging. Cordially and lovingly, she was asking Thad to shape-up his table manners.

How we criticize those we love and live with over an irritable behavior also has some significance in helping them change that bad habit. Going after a partner in a combatant way can potentially lead to them becoming defensive.

Whether or not Thad was aware of his lousy table manners, Lisa made it known that it existed and was a problem for her. She initiated a discussion on both the issue and what needs to be done (stop talking with mouth full of food) to solve the problem.

Like with all our differences, the key is, to be honest with each other when you have an issue with the other's behavior. Again, avoid becoming a complainer about every little thing because then you become the annoying one. Focus on addressing primarily those habits, quirks, and irritable behaviors that mainly stress you out. Also, find some time to strategize ways you can help each other change those irritating behaviors that bother each of you.

Sometimes you can make your partners poor behavior into a game which discourages them from a particular bad behavior. Using Thad's poor table manners as an example, maybe Lisa can arrange that every time he is caught talking with his mouth full of food, he must give Lisa 20 dollars. This will surely help discourage him from such behavior, given that it takes money out of his pocket and into Lisa's. But the key here is to change the bad behavior by discouraging it with creative disincentive methods.

Should You Move In Together?

Deciding whether to move in together with your partner is a personal decision. Both you and your partner must determine the real purpose for shacking up, especially if either or both have lived alone for an extended period. Is the reason for the move is to test you're living together relationship before marriage? Is it to save on living expenses?

Not everyone makes good roommates. And those that are among this group should think twice before taking the plunge to move in with their partner.

Also, couples should first give their relationship plenty of time of getting to know each other before shacking up or cohabitating. It's true; you learn more about a person when you live with them. But, it's better to gradually learn about your new partner during the traditional dating process. Dating is about getting to know each other better. How long should the dating process be before moving in with your partner or even getting married is up to the couple themselves. But whether it's cohabiting or getting married, neither move should be made until you both can say that you know, trust, and love each other well enough and are comfortable taking the relationship to the next step —shacking up together or marrying.

However, there are no guarantees that your relationship will last whether you decide to move in together or not. As we discussed in other chapters, people change over time. Couples grow apart in both cohabitation and marriage relationships.

So, before moving in with your partner, first, know yourself and then get to know your partner. Afterward, you will be better able to determine if shacking up would be more appropriate for you.

Shacking up Long-term? Consider a Cohabitation Contract

If you are entering a long cohabitation relationship, it would be wise to establish a written cohabitation contract. Such an agreement would give both parties legal control over the distribution of their property and finances. If the relationship broke up, the contract would be the focus of the litigation and not the personal reasons for the termination of the relationship.

Cohabitation Contracts cover many issues including title and interest to a specific real-estate; agreement with respect to business ventures, arrangements, or enterprises commenced or operated by the parties; agreement to comingle joint bank accounts or to maintain separate accounts; agreement with respect apartment leases and who gets the apartment in the event it goes co-op; and so many other issues that could be of concern should the relationship end and the parties go their separate ways.

Shacking up has become more popular among younger adults. According to 2018 U.S. Census report, those ages 18 to 24, 9 percent lived together with a partner as unmarried in 2018, compared with 7 percent living together as a married couple.

Key Points to Remember or Act Upon

- How we criticize those we live with over an irritable behavior also has some significance in helping them change that bad habit. Going after a partner in a combatant way can potentially lead to them becoming defensive.
- Focus on addressing primarily those habits, quirks, and annoying behaviors that mainly stress you out. Also, find some time to strategize ways you can help change each other's irritating conduct.
- Couples should first give themselves plenty of time of getting to know each other before shacking up or cohabitating. It's true; you learn more about a person when you live with them. But, it's better to gradually learn about your new partner during the traditional dating process.
- Before moving in with your partner, first, know yourself and then get to know your partner. Afterward, you will be better able to determine if shacking up would be appropriate for you.

Chapter 19

How to Be a Great French Kisser

Show me a woman that does not enjoy kissing her partner, and I'll show you a woman that has a lousy kissing partner. In general, women usually have a strong desire for physical closeness with their partner. This comes in the form of hand-holding, hugging, sitting close together, and most importantly, and kissing. According to research, many women use kissing as a bonding mechanism as well as a way to measure their partner's commitment to their relationship. However, the same can be said for men, but not as extensively. Still, women put a high value on kissing in a relationship. Therefore, for men who want to maintain a harmonious relationship or even grow that relationship if it's new; kiss your partner regularly. But this chapter is not about just any form of kissing; it's about French kissing—the most popular type of kissing for American lovers.

If you are a terrible French kisser, fear not. French kissing is an art form that can be learned. But before we get into the mechanics of French kissing, let's talk about the science of kissing in general.

The Science of Kissing

Our mouth and lips give out erotic pleasure. A kiss stimulates because it involves all the senses of touch, taste, and smell. Generally, love play begins with kissing, and when couples become more excited, the kisses become more intense and erotic. Many couples enjoy deep kissing where both lips and tongues meet. The penetration of the tongue into the other's mouth is analogous to the penetration of the penis into the vagina. Also, when two people kiss deeply with an open mouth, they exchange more than 10 million bacteria.

For humans, our lips are the body's most exposed erogenous zone, filled with sensitive nerves. The slightest brush sends a flow of information to our brains. Kissing also activates that part of brain associated with sensory information.

Kissing also sets off a cascade of neural impulses that bounce between the brain and the tongue, lips, facial muscles, and skin. You have more than a million nerve connections distributing information around the body, producing chemical signals that change the way we feel.

Such type of passionate kissing is associated with tongue action. This type of kissing can spike the neurotransmitter dopamine that is related to feelings of craving and desire.

When you are kissing someone passionately, a "love" hormone fosters a sense of closeness and attachment. Our heart rate is boosted by adrenaline, which can sometimes make us sweat. Also, the stress hormone can plunge, therefore, reducing uneasiness. Other internal activities that our bodies may undergo includes breathing becoming more profound, blood vessels dilating, cheeks becoming flush, and our pulse accelerating. And just think, all this internal body action is a result of a passionate or tongue-action kiss.

Of course, if you are not attracted to the person giving you a passionate kiss, it would not be a form of a turn-on; instead, the internal body action would be associated with repulsion and anger.

Stimulating kissing is not just associated with passionate kissing. A loving kiss from our partner on the cheek or mouth can also delicately and mildly bring on a sense of arousal.

Kissing your partner fosters the sensation we often describe with falling in love. It adds romance to the relationship while also bonding it. Also, it generates a deposit to your partner's Emotional Love Bank, as discussed earlier.

It Starts with a Clean Mouth

At one time or another, many men and women have had issues with some of their kissing partners. The first thing to do before kissing anyone, especially in the mouth, is to make sure your breath and teeth are clean. No one wants to kiss someone with bad breath and unclean teeth; regardless of how much you desire that person. Speaking from experience, I French kissed some women who breath was so unpleasant it killed the romantic mood. Simply put, it was a turn-off.

Therefore, always come prepared with a fresh breath when expecting or planning some serious kissing with your partner. For example, keep something like breath mints or gum as a precaution for what may become a romantic time with your partner. Also, when planning to spend some heavy kissing with your partner, avoid eating beforehand, foods like onion, garlic, and other foods that leave an unpleasant odor in your mouth.

As for your teeth, make sure there are no food particles visibly stuck between them and that they are clean. No one wants to French kiss someone and have their tongue touch food particles in your mouth or even worse transferred to their month. Also, brush and floss your teeth when you're expecting some romance time with your partner. This is common sense stuff, but I have heard many complaints from both men and women of kissing someone with bad breath or a filthy mouth.

Let's briefly stay on the subject of teeth for a moment. If your teeth are frequently bumping together during French kissing, that's a signal that you're doing something wrong. Avoid having your teeth clacking with your partner. In addition to teeth-rattling being both awkward and embarrassing; it can also sometimes be painful for those with sensitive teeth. However, unavoidably teeth can sometimes come together during kissing; try to keep it at a minimum.

How the Term French Kissing Came to Be

It varies how the term "French kissing" came to be. But the most popular one is that it originated from the English language around 1923 supposedly as a slur on the French culture that was believed to be excessively concerned with sex. In France, what we call French kiss is known as tongue kiss or soul kiss because it feels as though two souls are merging.

French Kissing 101

There are different styles of French kissing, and it can involve some 34 facial muscles. Different people may have a particular movement with their tongue than others. So, there is variety in how to French kiss. But there are some general steps you want to take when French kissing that is somewhat universal. So, whether you're male or female that is either new to French kissing, or it's been a while since you French kissed, the class is in session:

- **Lightly dampen your lips before going in for action.** Sweep your tongue over your lips before meeting your partner's lips. Another option, perhaps even better, would be to use lip balm before kissing your partner.
- **Approach real close.** Whether you're standing, sitting, or even lying down, come in close to each other's arms. You won't be able to do it well inches apart. And do whatever that comes naturally with your hands, such as holding hands, caressing, and touching your partner's face or neck.
- **Angle your head as you go in to give a kiss.** This is to avoid each other's noses from getting in the way during kissing. Make sure if your partner tilts his or her head to one side, you tilt your head to the opposite side for more

comfortable and deeper kissing. By the way, according to research, approximately two-thirds of people tilt their head to the right when kissing. But again, if your partner head tilts right when kissing, you lean left for a more soothing and easing kissing pattern.

- **Slowly brush your partner's lips.** Slightly open your lips and in between your lips keep your partner's lower or upper lip, and brush it slowly and softly.

- **(Optional) Close or slightly close your eyes as you begin kissing your partner.** Somehow kissing while your eyes are closed or partly closed, heighten the focus and sensation of the kiss. However, lovers also like to see the reaction of the person they are kissing. Therefore, do what comes naturally for you.

- **Open Lips slowly giving your partner a signal that you would like to French kiss**. If your partner open's their mouth in return, that's your invitation to proceed. But, if for example, you and your partner are in a new relationship and he or she is not ready for French kissing, respect their wishes. Instead, give them the closed mouth kiss; at least for now. Remember, kissing is a mutual desired participating affair.

- **Explore each other's tongue.** When and if you do get the green light from your partner that they are receptive to French kissing, slowly open your mouth and gently push your tongue into their mouth, without initially going too far inside. Start lightly, gently, and playfully touching each other's tongues. Continue slowly to get comfortable with your partner's mouth and tongue action. By the way, your partner will usually show their acceptance to French kissing by opening their mouth as you lead in opening yours.

- **Add variety to the kiss.** After getting accustomed to French kissing your partner, you may want to add some variety to your kissing such as using your tongue to kiss your partner deeper. Or you may want to mix the length of your kiss by kissing longer or shorter. Also, use your tongue to play with your partner's lips or make an O with your lips around your partner's tongue, and as you ease in apply a light suction.

- **Pay attention to your partner's reaction and body language**. During the time you're kissing, be aware of your partner's response, and make adjustments to your kissing accordingly. If, for example, your partner prefers a softer kiss, refrain from the heavy stuff. Part of being a great kisser is being able to read, please, and accommodate the kissing mood of your partner. Like sex, kissing is about pleasing your partner.

- **Develop and master your own kissing style.** As you and your partner become more accustom with French kissing, add your personal style and technique that brings more pleasure to you and your partner.

- **Remember to keep saliva at a minimum.** French kissing can sometimes tend to cause you to generate more saliva than you desire. Therefore, if you find yourself getting sloppy with excess spit from your saliva glands, simply swallow it while avoiding the breakup of the kiss. For some, this may take a little practice.

Because women generally place slightly higher value and importance on kissing than men, those men that are searching for women in the dating market would score high marks with them if they perfected their kissing technique. It will become a significant asset when they connect with the woman of their interest. Some reports say it is possible for some women actually to reach an orgasm through kissing. It would not surprise me if it were also possible for some men to have a similar reaction after a sensational passionate kiss.

Even some couples that have been in relationships for more extended periods can also use some kissing advice. For example, sometimes couples that have been in long-standing marriages or relationships can tend to forget how meaningful, simple things like kissing can be to their happiness. Some relationship experts advise such couples to engage in kissing each other every day for at least 10-second. The purpose is to get these couples back in the habit of kissing regularly.

Throughout history, kissing has always been a part of our culture. It is how we communicate with our partner lovingly and affectionately. It's also a form of foreplay before engaging in sex.

Just like sex, kissing should be a fun experience. Therefore, practice and perfect these French kissing suggestions, and you should make your partner a happy and willingly participant in the art of French kissing.

Be a Safe French Kisser

Keep in mind that certain diseases are transmittal through kissing with an open mouth. Among those diseases include mononucleosis "kissing disease," herpes, and HIV.

Because you are exchanging saliva during French kissing, you could become infected with a person, for example, who has the HIV virus. The virus in your partner's saliva could enter your body if you have a cut on the inside of your mouth. Therefore, know your partner's HIV and other disease status before getting into deep open mouth kissing. Also, make sure neither you nor your partner has open cuts in your mouth if one or both of you have a transmittable disease.

Kissing should be both enjoyable and safe.

Key Points to Remember or Act Upon

- Kissing your partner fosters the sensation we often describe with falling in love. It adds romance to the relationship while also bonding it. Also, it generates a deposit to your partner's Emotional Love Bank.
- The first thing to do before kissing anyone, especially in the mouth, is to make sure your breath and teeth are clean. No one wants to kiss someone with bad breath and unclean teeth; regardless of how much you desire that person.
- When and if you do get the green light from your partner that they are receptive to French kissing, slowly open your mouth and gently push your tongue into their mouth, without going too far inside initially. Start lightly, gently and playfully touching each other's tongues.
- After getting use to French kissing your partner, you may want to add some variety to your kissing such as using your tongue to kiss your partner deeper. Or you may want to mix the length of your kiss by kissing longer or shorter.
- During the time you're kissing, be aware of your partner's response and make adjustments to your kissing accordingly. If, for example, your partner prefers a softer kiss, refrain from the heavy stuff. Part of being a great kisser is being able to read, please, and accommodate the kissing mood of your partner.

Chapter 20

Evaluating Your Marriage Potential and Making Marriage Successful

Go onto several dating sites and read some of the profiles and you will find many singles on these sites are interested in getting married. It's a mixture of those have been married before and those that have never wedded. Some give a reason why they want to get married while many do not. What is clear is that the marriage institution is still alive and well in American culture. It does not matter whether you been through one or more failed marriages; many still want to be in a traditional marriage relationship. Besides, marriage has its benefits, among the advantages, are financial, legal, psychological, and security-related.

However, before you seriously considering marrying, ask yourself some important key questions to help determine if you are ready for marriage. You should respond candidly to all questions regarding your marriage preparedness. Your responses to specific questions will help you assess your actual readiness for tying the knot to matrimony.

But before we get into what questions you should ask and respond to, let's talk about the marriage institution itself.

The Institution of Traditional Marriage

Traditional marriage has been around for a long time. When I refer to traditional marriage, I'm speaking of marriage between a man and a woman. Not same-sex marriage, which I personally do not recognize as a real marriage. But I digress. Traditional marriage is a sacred thing, and despite the reasons why people marry can vary; marriage is the foundation for having children and raising a family. Through marriage, a man and woman spiritually, legally and emotionally become one.

Also, when a man and woman marry their relationship often is based on inter-dependence. Each satisfies essential needs of the other person, whether it's emotionally, financially, sexually, or other means. Marriage is about being committed to your spouse, not only during good times but also bad times. When a man and woman marry, they are an entire team. They become a unit made up of many parts. Their faith, marriage, and family are at the top of their list of what's most important to them.

Based upon marriage sacredness and the life-changing results, deciding on whether you should marry and, if so, who you marry is one of the most important decisions you will ever make. Therefore, it makes sense to tread carefully when making choices about marriage.

Some people are not the marrying type. If this is you; the most natural decision is not to get hitched. However, if you are the marrying type; make sure that the person you seek to marry is compatible with you. Give yourself plenty of time to get to know that person and allow that person to get to know you. Six months is not enough time to get to know someone. Yes, you may fall in love with that person way before six months, but do you truly know them? Have you seen them in different situations that portray other characteristics about themselves? Have you had adequate time to resolve some of your differences?

To get to know someone and feel comfortable in deciding on whether you want to marry them; you should take at least a year spending time learning about each other. A year is not an eternity. As a matter-of-fact, these days a year seems to go by fast. Therefore, spend that time getting to know each other like never before. If you both are confident that you are right for each other and are committed to marriage; get engaged! If at least a year has elapsed from the time you began dating; then make your marriage plans.

Just like many other things in life, there are no guarantees in marriage. Some married couples had a short courtship for far less than a year and have been married 50, 60 or more years. Therefore, there are exceptions to my "one-year get to know rule before marriage."

Also, it pays to learn from others who had successful marriages. For example, my parents remained married to each other for the remainder of their life. Sure they had their number of arguments, including some that became slightly physical. But their marriage survived because they were committed to their marriage and loved each other unconditionally.

The same unconditional love applied to my late grandparent's marriage. As a young child, I learned what true unconditional love and marriage meant when I watched my grandmother tirelessly and faithfully nursed my dying grandfather around the clock. My grandfather was in his early 60s when he became ill from bone cancer. I watched my grandmother feed, bath, and sat-up late at night with him throughout his illness. It was one of the greatest and prominent displays of love and affection for one's spouse in sickness that I had ever witnessed at such an early age.

RELATIVES WEDDING PHOTO: Like family reunions and funerals, weddings tend to bring together relatives and friends. This photo was taken in 1951, more than three years before I was born. My mother, the Maid of Honor, is standing next to the bride. My grandmother is on the left, behind the bride, barely visible. My grandfather is in the far back row, third from right.

If you want a healthy marriage, you are going to have to work hard at it, meaning giving it constant attention. Like a house that needs on-going upkeep, so does a marriage requires similar attention and care. As issues come up that may cause relationship friction; couples need to repair or resolve such problems to avoid a breakdown in the relationship.

Few marriages regardless of how strong they are will ever be exempt from problems—it comes with being in a relationship with another person. Learn to resolve or tolerate issues that occur in a marriage and continue to live in harmony with each other. Your marriage requires caring for your spouse that you pledged to cherish for the rest of your life. As life-long partners, you should be willing and able to confront and resolve whatever obstacles or challenges that come your way. Such problem-solving approach is what strengthens a marriage. But, for any marriage to be successful, both husband and wife must be committed to making it work— without any exceptions!

Taking Inventory of Your Marital Preparedness

Earlier in this chapter, I challenged you to ask yourself some tough questions before seriously considering marriage. Depending on your honest response to such questions, you should be able to determine whether or not you are truly ready for marriage. There is no right or wrong responses to these questions. They are designed to measure or reflect your real preparedness and desire for marriage.

Below are 20 questions. On a separate sheet of paper, respond to the following questions as honestly and specific as possible:

1. **What are the challenges one will have living with you regularly (List, for example, bad habits, behaviors that may be annoying to others, etc.)?**

2. **Identify all the reasons why you want to get married.**

194

3. If you were married before and later divorced, what, if anything, did you learned from that failed marriage?

4. How will you apply what you learned from your failed marriage to your next marriage so that it also does not end in divorce?

5. Before marrying, are you willing to be honest with your future spouse about yourself, including your history, finances, past relationships, etc.?

6. What, if anything, about your future spouse would make you reconsider marrying that person?

7. Do you have a craving to have sex or be in a romantic relationship with other men or women, despite having a desire to get married to one person?

8. Do you have any baggage that you are currently dealing with in past relationships that need to resolve before entering a marriage? If so, what are they and what plans, if any, you will put in place to reduce or eliminate such baggage?

9. How will you resolve a situation when you want to relocate to a new town, but your future spouse is hesitant to do so?

10. If your future spouse asks that you sign a prenuptial agreement before you marry; are you willing to do so?

11. If you ask your future spouse to sign a prenuptial agreement before your wedding, but he or she refuses to do so; are you still willing to proceed with the marriage?

12. If your future spouse has huge debt issues before your marrying, are you willing to help pay down on those debts?

13. What, if anything, you are most nervous about in getting married?

14. What, if anything, you are most excited and happy about in getting married?

15. On a scale of 1 to 10 with 10 being the highest, how would you rank yourself mentally or psychologically as being ready for marriage and why?

16. On a scale of 1 to 10 with 10 being the highest, how would you rank yourself financially prepared for marriage and why?

17. How long have you had a desire to get married?

18. Are you opened to have children born from your married?

19. How long are you willing to wait before getting married?

20. What if anything you are not willing to compromise on in a marriage?

Review your responses and assess where you are (based upon your answers) in terms of being ready for marriage. You may also want to add and respond to other questions not included above. Regardless of how you responded to the questions, if you are in a relationship with someone that you are considering marrying, you should share your responses with them. Have candid discussions about your answers. Also, invite them to respond to the same questions. It's a great way to measure their readiness for marriage or show whether or not you are both on the same page about marriage.

Marriage is a major decision we make in our lives. Whatever tools we use to help us prepare and assess our readiness for marriage, regardless of our age and frequency of marriage, is worth using.

Marry if you are Committed, Prepared and Found Your Compatible Match

There are many decisions we make in life that will have a profound effect on our destiny; marriage is one of them. When you and your spouse-to-be decide to marry, not only are you both making a significant personal decision, but also a legal one. From the day the minister announces you both husband and wife; you are expected to be as one. A lifetime partnership in sickness and in health, and until death do you part. But even in death, the expectations are that you, and your spouse remains will be buried side-by-side.

Given the impact that marriage will have on your life, it's only appropriate that you are confident that the person you are marrying is compatible with you. I cannot overstress how important this is to the success of a marriage. The expectation is you and your partner will share similar values and beliefs. A significant degree of chemistry should also exist in your relationship, whether it is in communication, overall behavior, or other areas. As I discussed in Chapters 1 and 15, you should also honestly be able to say to each other that you are best friends. When you can both sincerely say these things about each other; you have most likely found your compatible match.

Many couples found their compatible match, but are not necessarily married. For one or more reasons, they decided not to tie the knot. Perhaps they realize that one or both were not the marrying type. Or maybe they didn't want to be tied down by a legal document. The reasons for not getting married are as many as there are reasons for getting married. Some couples have been together, but unmarried, for several decades and have no intentions of ever marrying.

If you found your compatible match and are willing to tie the knot with that person, you still need to acknowledge whether you both are committed to and prepared for marriage. If couples can genuinely say yes to being both committed and prepared for marriage; then I believe they should move forward and wed.

However, let's define what being committed and prepared for marriage mean.

For a marriage to thrive, the couple must be committed to giving it time and attention throughout its duration. A couple must be willing to put much energy into making the marriage work. There must be a commitment to have honest and open communications with each other, which both partners respectfully listens to the other. There must be a commitment by both partners to make their marriage a priority. Yes, there will be plenty of difficult times ahead, but they must have the attitude that nothing will get in the way of making their marriage work. Not the in-laws, children, money issues, health matters, or anything else will break up their marriage. Again, marriage is something that requires constant work. There will be times when the relationship will encounter some significant challenges that may put into question whether the marriage can go on. You and your spouse must have the attitude and approach that without a doubt you both will remain man and wife. Whatever conflicts there are, regardless of how difficult and dire, you both as a couple will work through them together. This is what is meant by being committed to your marriage. You not only have an attitude of the marriage commitment, but your actions reflect that dedication to your relationship.

Marriage preparedness is related to commitment. In being prepared for marriage, you take the responsibility to adapt to developmental changes in each other. There must be continued efforts and desires to make your partner feel cherished, loved, needed, appreciated, and respected. If you have not been good at managing your finances or you have not saved enough for retirement or other purposes, you could face money problems later or sooner in a marriage. If you are not financially capable of paying your bills, this could result in some money issues in your marriage. Discuss with your spouse-to-be each others' opinions about saving, money management philosophies, and spending habits. You want to have some idea of how you both will manage your money during the marriage. For example, will you have separate and joint banking accounts? Will only one of you be responsible for the household finances? What percentage will each be responsible for paying the bills? Do you need to have a prenuptial agreement? These and many other questions need to be discussed and decided on before marriage. Also, share each other's credit scores, debts, and other money matters that you both need to be aware of as a couple. This helps to ensure there are no surprises when, for example, you attempt to take out a loan for a house or other big-ticket item. These are all types of information sharing that will help you better prepared for your marriage. There should be no secrets when you go into a marriage. Besides, you are supposed to be marrying your best friend, your better half, the person that will always have your back as you will have theirs.

Should You Have a Prenuptial Agreement?

Prenuptial agreements are a touchy subject for many couples going into a marriage. However, there have been surveys showing such agreements are increasing among couples. For example, prenuptial agreements seem to be on the rise among couples that were previously married one or more times before or have children from a previous marriage. Prenuptial agreements also seem to increase among couples which one partner is exceptionally wealthy than the other.

Prenuptial agreements can be emotionally difficult for some couples. However, it can avoid some of the hurt caused by a painful divorce where both parties are fighting over asset values and their distribution.

A prenuptial agreement is a legal document that describes how property and assets both bought into and acquired during a marriage will be treated should a divorce occur. Despite the rise in prenuptial agreements, they are not for everyone getting married. For example, a young couple getting married for the first time having little or no assets may not need such an agreement. But a prenuptial arrangement does make good business sense if that same young couple individually has an inheritance or trust from their parents or other relatives. Other reasons when it may be advisable to draw up a prenuptial agreement before getting married is when significant assets are involved, such as a home, stock, or retirement fund. Also, a prenuptial agreement may be needed when one or both partners own all or part of a business before their marriage.

One partner, usually the one which has lesser assets at stake, may feel a bit of resentment from their partner wanting a prenuptial agreement. He or she may feel as though the other does not have faith in their marriage or lack trust in them. Here is where the couple needs to discuss their differences and come to a resolution. Many times the person seeking the agreement will need to convince their partner its purpose, benefits, and how it has no reflection on their love for each other. The key is to look upon the prenuptial agreement as an "insurance policy" to avert the costly expenses of litigation when a marriage ends.

A disagreement on a prenuptial agreement does not have to result in the cancellation of a wedding. Like all tough decisions a married couple makes when there are disagreements, there must be some room for compromising. Understand why your partner feels one way about an issue. Put yourself in his or her shoes. Seek out ways so that each may have a win-win situation. Agreeing on a prenuptial agreement can be emotionally challenging, but it's one among many other tough decisions you will make as a couple prior to marriage and during marriage.

Final Thoughts about Marriage

Traditional marriage is a great institution provided that you are in a marriage with a person that is compatible with you and makes your life complete. Few things are more significant than having someone special to share your life. You are lovers and best friends for life and can depend upon each other without hesitation.

But by no means is marriage easy. It requires constant work. Here are samples of many things you must do to keep your marriage healthy, exciting, and until death do you depart:

- Regularly fit in little acts of kindness in your relationship with your spouse. For example, let your spouse sleep in late some Saturday mornings while you fix breakfast for the kids. Make sure you save some breakfast for your spouse after they wake up.
- Send through U.S. mail a special love letter to your spouse. He or she will be pleasantly surprised. Make sure the letter is handwritten. This makes it extra personalized.
- Make it a common practice to boost your spouse mood. For example, if they seem stressed or downed, hug or kiss them. Tell them how much you love and appreciated them. Make them laugh or smile during those times when they may be in a sad or bad mood.
- Spend time apart. Married couples need to retain their identity so they won't feel smothered. Yes, you are a team, but you also are individuals. Therefore, allow each other to grow as individuals while retaining the closeness of your marriage. Being a complete person makes you a happier person.
- Regardless of how busy your schedule is, always carve out some time with your spouse for conversation, activity, or merely bonding time. This includes going out on dates regularly.
- Always be honest and open with each other.
- Take wonderful vacations together to places you both never been before.

A marriage is what you put into it. These are just a few of the great ways you and your spouse can make a beautiful and adventurous life together.

Key Points to Remember or Act Upon

- Marriage is about being committed to your spouse, not only during good times but also bad times. When a man and woman marry, they are an entire team. They become a unit made up of many parts. Their faith, marriage, and family are at the top of their list of what's most important to them.

- Some people are not the marrying type. If this is you; the easiest decision is not to get hitched. However, if you are the marrying type; make sure that the person you seek to marry is compatible with you. Give yourself plenty of time to get to know that person and allow that person to get to know you.

- Prenuptial agreements can be emotionally difficult for some couples. However, it can avoid some of the hurt caused by a painful divorce where both parties are fighting over asset values and their distribution.

- To determine your readiness for marriage, respond honestly to the 20 questions in this chapter on marriage preparedness. Also (if applicable), ask the person you are considering marrying to respond to the same questions.

Conclusion

Many of our grandparents, other older relatives, and to some extent our parents, depending on their age, met their spouse or mate at high school, college, work, church, a party, or some other place or event. Today, thanks to the Internet and online dating, the opportunities of singles meeting or finding each other has expanded. As a result of the Internet and the growth of online dating, eventually, someday, we arguably are likely to meet our future mate on a dating site almost as equally as meeting them in more conventional ways such as at a social event or the local neighborhood singles bar.

Despite online dating growth, some are still timid about telling others that they met their new mate on a dating site. For example, if such a couple was at a party and someone asked them where or how they met, they may hesitate to respond that they met on a dating site. However, with the popularity of online dating, many are becoming more comfortable with telling their friends and relatives that they met on Match.com, ChristianMingle.com, or any of the other popular dating sites. It may not sound as romantic as telling someone you met at the park on a summer afternoon or at a ballroom dance show, but where you met is not as important as that you found each other.

Online dating is part of the match-making culture we live in today, and it does not look like it's a fad that will disappear anytime soon. It provides singles with an option to offline ways of meeting potential partners. Its popularity has made it a profitable business to be a part of in a growing population of singles and devoice people, not only in America but also worldwide.

Had it not been for the Internet and online dating, many of the people from 1995 to today may not have ever met or married. It is the Internet and online dating that has opened up the world to us to meet others that we would not have known existed otherwise. This is one of the great ways we have benefited from both the Internet and online dating.

Yes, there are some unscrupulous and dishonest characters on dating sites, but there are also some friendly and sincere people as well. Your job as a member of these dating sites is to distinguish the unpleasant users from the more pleasant ones. Carefully view profiles and establish conversations with those people that you like, have a common interest, or share compatibility.

We are fortunate to live in an age which the Internet and online dating has exploded. Thanks to the Internet technology and growth of online dating, singles have the capability of finding a mate more easily provided they are willing to put in the effort.

If you found the love of your life already, be grateful and continue to do the things that make your relationship happy and fruitful. Chances are you are doing some of the things I spoke about in this book on developing your relationship, and are doing them well.

However, if you are still searching for that elusive person to help make your life more complete, consider taking advantage of the opportunities online dating offers along with offline options. The key is to use both online and offline options available to you for finding a compatible mate. Also, make yourself accessible and visible to potential mates by utilizing both online and offline opportunities. Women and men with similar interest, whether it is tennis, ballroom dancing, skating or whatever, need to hangout where such activities and events take place. They are bound to meet each other since they are at a place or event that they share a common interest. Having discussions of similar interests with those online is another way of making a connection with someone potentially a good match for you. After getting to know each other a bit more online, you can later arrange a date to participate in a shared interest such as biking, hiking, or bowling.

Although there are plenty of online sites that require you to pay a fee to join, there are also a variety of free online dating sites. Use both, if necessary, for finding your mate. Carefully read members profiles to get familiar with who they are and how they compare to what you are looking for in a mate. Even if they say little in their profile, consider contacting them with a greeting to help get a conversation going so you can learn more about them.

If you are serious about finding your compatible match online, carefully read, and apply the ideas I offer on how to post your profile in Chapter 5. How you display your profile has a reflection of how viewers perceive you. For example, blurry photos or a written profile with several misspelled words could leave viewers with a negative impression of you. Therefore, when posting your profile, ask yourself, how will others perceive you? Will they look upon you positively or negatively? Also, if your profile is not attracting the type of persons you are seeking, consider modifying it so that it draws the attention of those that interest you.

When you do finally meet your match, put into practice some of the methods, techniques, and ideas I shared with you throughout this book for enhancing your relationship. I'm very confident they will help you develop your relationship so that you and your match or spouse can live in harmony with each other. They will also set an example for your kids on what a loving relationship looks like as you become relationship role models to them.

I was inspired to write this book for many reasons. Among those were the many people I encounter online sharing their frustration and difficulty in finding the right person for them. I was also motivated in writing this book by the many happy couples and relatives that I knew that had long-term, prosperous relationships and marriages. There were many reasons why their relationships were thriving and successful, and I wanted to share some of them to inspire others that are seeking something similar.

Writing this book was also somewhat therapeutic for me. I had beautiful relationships, despite some not always being long-term. I periodically shared some of my personal experiences to expand on the various points I was making on a particular topic.

After reading this book, don't just put it down and not put some of the ideas and methods discussed into practice. For example, the Compatibility Point Factor Chart is a wonderful tool for helping you to identify your match on dating sites. It can also be used with potential partners you meet offline. Also, make it a practice to use the concept of making continuous deposits to your partner's Emotional Love Bank. You are sure to receive a continuous positive and favorable reaction from them in return.

Like any new information learned, to make it useful and beneficial, you need to put into practice, so it becomes part of your lifestyle. Highlight key points in the book that interest you or you want to apply to your relationships. Use it as a resource or even motivator in keeping your relationship healthy, romantic, and exciting.

I wish you well in both finding your compatible mate and building or maintaining a successful long-term relationship!

Notes

Preface:

1. Information when Great Expectations was founded retrieved from https://en.wikipedia.org/wiki/Timeline_of_online_dating_services (July 19, 2019).
2. Martin Zwilling (March 1, 2013), How Many More Dating Sites Do We Need, Forbes Magazine.
3. The Match Group: Dating Revenue 2018, Source: Statista.

Chapter 1:   Six Factors That Identify Your Potential Match

1. Justin C. Scott, (May 21, 2017) The Difference Between Compatibility and Chemistry.
2. Jonathan Small, (2016), 5 Kinds of Chemistry: Have You Felt Them All? Chemistry.com.

Chapter 2:   Knowing Your Non-Compromising Needs from Your Compromising Needs

1. Jessica Reynolds, (July 12, 2015), Relationship deal breakers and when they really matter, Chicago Tribune, pp 4-5.

Chapter 4:   Selecting the Best Dating Sites for Long-Term Relationships

1. Craig Smith (August 9, 2019), Interesting Match.com Statistics and Facts by the Numbers. Retrieved from https://expandedramblings.com/index.php/matchcom-statistics-and-facts/
2. Information on eharmony.com retrieved from https://www.eharmony.com/about/eharmony/.

Notes

Chapter 5:   **Ways to Post Profiles That Attract Your Potential Match**

1. Alicia McElhaney (Sept 1, 2013) Online dating? Don't Underestimate the Photo, McClatchy Newspapers.
2. Marisa Meltzer, (Feb. 2017) Match Me IF You Can, *Craft a Profile with Polish*, p 41, CR.Org.
3. Ron Geraci (June 2002) Looking to Click, *Don't Look like a Loser Online*, p 125, Men's Health.

Chapter 8:   **How to Identify and Avoid Scammers on Dating Websites**

1. Margarette Burnette, (Oct. 8, 2017), Actions to Take If Your Account is in Jeopardy, Nerd Wallet.
2. *FBI*.gov (Feb 7, 2018) FBI Cautions Public to be Wary of Online Romance Scams, FBI Washington Office of Public Affairs.
3. Information on Google Images retrieved from Images.Google.com
4. Information on Social Catfish retrieved from SocialCatfish.com
5. Information on Beenverified retrieved fromBeenverified.com

Chapter 9:   **Some Contemporary Dating Apps and Sites with Different Concepts**

1. Erin Barry, (Feb 10, 2018) On This Dating App, Every One is a "Hater" and it Brings People Together, On the Money.
2. https://bumble.com/
3. https://onlinehookupsites.com/meld-dating-app-review/
4. https://www.happn.com/
5. Amber Brooks, (Sept. 7, 2017) SparkStarter: A Free Dating App in Minneapolis Invites Your Friends to Play Matchmaker & Make Introductions, Dating Advice.com.
6. Christopher Doering, (June 11, 2016), TrumpSingles: 'Making Dating Great Again,' USAToday.
7. https://settleforlove.com/

Notes

Chapter 10:   First and Second Dates Are Learning Opportunities

1. Jenniffer Weigel (Dec. 18, 2011) Watch Your Language Tribune Newspapers.
2. Jessica Reynolds (Feb. 8, 2015) Has Google Changed 1st Dates? pp 4-5, Chicago Tribune.

Chapter 11:   Should You Date or Marry Someone Much Older or Younger Than You?

1. Stefan Bechtel, Laurence Roy Stains, and Editors of Men's Health Books, *Older Men, Younger Women*, (1996), Sex A Man's Guide, Rodale Press, Inc.
2. Stefan Bechtel, Laurence Roy Stains, and Editors of Men's Health Books, *Younger Men, Older Women*, (1996), Sex A Man's Guide, Rodale Press, Inc.
3. Information on Elvis and Priscilla Presley retrieved from https://en.wikipedia.org/wiki/Priscilla_Presley
4. Jerry L. Lewis https://en.wikipedia.org/wiki/Jerry_Lee_Lewis

Chapter 12:   Should You Date or Marry Someone of a Different Race?

1. Kristen Bialik, (June 12, 2017), Key Facts About Race and Marriage, 50 Years After Loving v. Virginia.
2. 2015 Statistics Source: Pew Research Center.

Chapter 13:   Should You Date Only Those that Share Your Political Ideology?

1. Michael Morell, (Feb. 11, 2014), Survival Tips From a Political Odd Couple, U.S. News & World Report.
2. https://www.gopatrio.com/
3. https://www.republicanpeoplemeet.com/
4. https://www.conservativedatingsite.com/
5. https://www.republicanpassions.com/
6. https://www.democraticpeoplemeet.com/

7. https://www.democratsingles.com/
8. https://liberalhearts.com/
9. https://www.datingadvice.com/

Chapter 14: Attractions that Appeal to us in Dating and Relationships

1. Tiffany Bailey (July 13, 2019). What Are The Different Types of Attraction and What Do They Mean?

Chapter 15: 20 Must Have Qualities to Maintain a Strong Relationship

1. Elizabeth Bernstein, (Oct. 4, 2011), Putting the Honey Back in 'Honey, I'm Home, *The Witching Hour: Rules of Engagement*, p D4, The Wall Street Journal.
2. Brett & Kate McKay (May 8, 2008), How Do You Know When She's the One, The Art of Manliness
3. D.A. Benton, (2003), Executive Charisma, Be Human, Humorous, and Hands On, *Be Humorous*, McGraw Hill.
4. Willard F. Harley, Jr. (May 1994), His Needs Her Needs, The First Thing She Can't Do Without, *Affection,* Fleming H. Revell.
5. Brian Tracy, (1993), Maximum Achievement, *Six Rules For Successful Relationships*, Simon & Schuster.

Chapter 16: To Enhance Your Relationship Increase Emotional Love Bank Deposits

1. Willard F. Harley, Jr. (May 1994), His Needs Her Needs, Why *Your Love Bank Never Closes, pp 18-22, Fleming H. Revell*
2. Stephen R. Covey, (2004), The 7 Habits of Highly Effective, *The Emotional Bank Account, pp 188-190, Free Press.*

Chapter17: Factors That Make Long-Distance Relationships Successful

1. Richard Asa, (Oct. 13, 2013), When Romance Starts with Lots of Mileage, pp 10-11, Chicago Tribune.
2. Anne Amore, (2011), Successful Long Distance Relationships – The 7 Key Secrets of Successful Long Distance Relationships, EzineArticles.com.

Chapter 18:   Making a Relationship Work While Shacking Up

1. Alexia Elejalde-Ruiz, (July 11, 2010), Living Together, Loving Together, Divorcing Together, Tribune Newspapers.
2. Amanda Eisenberg (June 22, 2014), Living Together Means Living with Pet Peeves Too, p 13,Chicago Tribune.
3. Nicole Anzia, (Aug. 6, 2017) Lay Down Your Arms, pp 18-19, Chicago Tribune.

Chapter 19:   How to Be a Great French Kisser

1. Laura Berman, (Sept. 10, 2007), Starting a Romance? Use Pucker Power, Chicago Sun-Times.
2. Sheril Kirshenbaum (Dec. 21, 2014), A Kiss is Not Just a Kiss, pp 4-5, Chicago Tribune.
3. French Kissing steps http://www.wikihow.com/French-Kiss
4. Stefan Bechtel, Laurence Roy Stains, and Editors of Men's Health, (1996), *Kissing, The Passion of the Lips*, Sex A Man's Guide, Rodale Press, Inc.

Chapter 20:   Evaluating Your Marriage Potential and Making Marriage Successful

1. Dave Carpenter, (May 30, 2010), Till Prenup Do US Part, The Associated Press.
2. Cheryl L. Young (March 2, 2015) Prenuptial Agreement a Must for Most Couples? *It May Not Be Fun, But It Can Save A Lot of Heartache*, p R4, The Wall Street Journal.
3. Steven Mitchell Sack, (1987), The Complete Legal Guide to Marriage, Divorce, Custody, and Living Together, *Prenuptial Agreements*, McGraw-Hill.

Index